Timeless Tailoring

Ready-to-Wear Techniques

Second Edition

Timeless Tailoring
Ready-to-Wear Techniques

Second Edition

Starr M Hashiguchi

Hamler Wilson LLC, 16011 SE 253rd Place, Covington, WA 98042-4195

Copyright © 2021, 1994 Starr M Hashiguchi

All rights reserved. Second Edition

ISBN: 978-0-578-84391-9

DEDICATION

Dedicated to my husband, Hachiro, my children, Mia, Aya and Ko, my grandchildren, Keiko, Tim, David, Connie, Kieran and Morgan and my great grandchildren, Ruth and June.

TABLE OF CONTENTS

Acknowledgments.................................... ix
Introduction 1
Tools and Equipment 2
  Pattern Adjustment Tools 2
  Tools for Cutting and Marking 2
  Pressing Equipment 2
The Tailored Jacket 7
  Pattern Selection 7
  Fabric Selection 8
    Fashion Fabric 8
    Lining Fabric 8
    Interfacing 8
      Interfacing Types 8
      Interfacing Selection 9
  Fabric Preparation 9
    Pretreating Wools and Wool Blends 9
    Lining Fabric Preparation 9
    Fusible Interfacing Preparation 9
  Choosing and Applying Fusible Interfacing 10
    Jacket Interfacing Weights 10
    How to Apply Fusible Interfacing 11
  Jacket Pattern Preparation 11
    Jacket Front 12
    Jacket Back 13
    Front Facing 13
    Back Neck Facing 14
    Sleeves 14
    Collar 14
    Patch Pocket 14
  Lining Pattern Preparation 15
    Front Lining 15
    Back Lining 15
    Back Lining (If You Added a Vent) 16
    Sleeve Lining 17
    Patch Pocket Lining 17

Interfacing Pattern Preparation 17
  Front 17
  Front Facing 18
  Patch Pocket 18
  Hems 18
  Vents 18
  Collars 18
Cutting and Preparing to Sew the Jacket 18
  Cutting the Jacket and Lining Pieces ... 18
  Cutting and Applying the Interfacing Pieces.. 18
  Marking 20
Jacket and Lining Construction 21
  Preparing for Stitching 21
  Pressing 23
  Patch Pocket Assembly 23
  Collar Assembly 23
  Sleeve Assembly (with Mock Vents) ... 24
  Sleeves with Vents 25
  Pocket Application 26
  Center Back Vent 26
  Attaching the Facings 29
  Adding the Collar 30
  Fitting the Lining to the Jacket 31
  Inserting the Sleeves 32
    Alternate Method for Sleeve Insertion 33
  Finishing the Jacket 33
Jacket Pockets 34
  Double Welt Pockets 36
    Cutting 36
    Construction 36
  Flap Pocket 39
    Cutting 39
    Construction 39
  Inside-Stitched Patch Pocket 42
    Cutting and Construction 42

- Alternate Patch Pocket Method 44
  - Inside Jacket Pocket 44
    - *Cutting* 44
    - *Construction* 44

The Tailored Coat, Simplified 49
Fabric Selection 49
- Fashion Fabric 49
- Lining Fabric 49
- Interlining and Underlining 49
- Other Support Fabrics 50

Coat Pattern Preparation 50
- Buttonhole Placement 50
- Pocket Placement 51
- Upper Collar 51
- Undercollar 51
- Lapel 51
- Lining 51
- Interfacing 51

Fabric Preparation, Layout and Cutting 52
Marking 53
- Tailor Tacks 53
- Mark Stitches 53
- Snip Marks 53

First Fitting 54
- First Fitting Checklist 54

Buttonholes and Pockets 54

Interfacing Preparation 55
- Darts 55
  - *Method One* 55
  - *Method Two* 55

Applying Edge Tape and Padstitching the Interfacing 55
Interfacing Application 56
- Applying Hymo to the Coat Front 56
- Padstitching the Hymo 56
- Attaching the Edge Tape 59
- Applying the Back Interfacing 60
- Interfacing the Undercollar 61

Attaching the Undercollar 62
Sleeve Assembly and Insertion 63
Assembling the Lining 64
Attaching the Upper Collar to the Facing 65
Sewing the Lining/Facing Unit to the Coat 66
Hemming the Coat and the Lining 67
Securing the Loose Ends 67
Finishing 68
Coat Pockets 70
- Vertical Welt Pockets 70
  - *Pattern Preparation* 71
  - *Cutting* 72
  - *Construction* 72

Sources 74
Bibliography 74
Pocket Patterns 75
About the Author 83

ACKNOWLEDGEMENTS

First and foremost, my gratitude to the Director of the Muramatsu School of Dressmaking and Design in Nagoya, Japan, Umee Muramatsu, who personally gave of her time and expertise so that I could cram in as much as I could of techniques used in Japan. Mr. Stanley Hostek, for his inspiration and sharing of the traditional tailoring techniques in his classes at the College. To Judy Barlup, who uses this method in her tailoring classes taught around the Pacific Northwest, to Camila Sigelmann and Jane Whiteley for their contributions. To the Instructors and Students of the Apparel Design Program at Seattle Central Community College for their encouragement and support. To editor, Barbara Weiland, and Kay Green, Designer, for their valuable advice and much needed aid. To my family, especially, husband Hachiro, for their moral support and love, I am eternally, grateful.

INTRODUCTION

Traditional tailoring requires much time-consuming and careful hand work to achieve the desired qualities. It is still sought after by discriminating dressers who can afford the investment of custom-made clothing and by those who have the time to do the fine work for themselves. A custom tailored garment is characterized by excellent fit, careful and accurate construction, and permanent shaping and durability achieved with the appropriate inner support fabrics for the desired look.

Modern ready-to-wear tailored garments are now constructed mostly by machine. With the availability of high-quality fusible interfacings and notions, much of the necessity for hand sewing has been eliminated. If you are a student preparing for a career in the fashion industry or a home sewer wishing to make garments with the ready-to-wear look, learning the methods used by manufacturers is essential.

The material presented in this book will help you achieve the ready-to-wear look, using factory-like construction methods and pattern changes. Construction is done in units to save time and eliminate over-handling of the garment pieces. Not all handwork has been eliminated. It is used where necessary to enhance the wearing quality and appearance of the garment.

I learned the methods presented in this book over a fourteen-month period in 1979 and 1980. I accompanied my husband to Japan where he was on assignment with the Boeing Company to work on the development of the Boeing 767 airplane. Knowing that there would be much time to fill during the day, I decided to do some research and to learn different sewing techniques and teaching methods that would be useful when I returned home to the US. To that end, I visited a number of schools of fashion in the city of Nagoya to find one that would fit my needs. I chose the Muramatsu School because the director there allowed me to enroll on a part-time basis to take selected classes, rather than requiring me to enroll as a full-time student following a prescribed course of studies. This school also offered classes in traditional Japanese sewing, which was a completely new field for me to explore—a real plus!

Among the classes taught by the director was one using manufacturing methods. It stressed not only time- and work-saving construction techniques, but also methods using different seam widths than those commonly found in commercial patterns. The value of changing seam widths in order to better control the garment edges, lapels, and collar was one of the most important things I learned and will share with you as you use this book. It is critical to the finished appearance of a tailored garment.

The director of the school, who is a well-known educator and personality in the Japanese fashion field, also gave me entry to several manufacturers and suppliers in order to observe and to take advantage of available information and goods. I found that manufacturers in Japan produce top quality goods for demanding consumers. There are no outlet stores to sell seconds because any flawed or incorrectly constructed part of a garment is promptly recut and replaced. Garments are not done completely by machine, but have touches of hand work in areas that need special handling. Though the bottom line for the manufacturers is making a profit, they do not sacrifice quality or customer satisfaction for quick profits.

What I learned about ready-to-wear tailoring in Japan is included in this book. You will find that these methods are not one of the "quick-and-easy" methods, but a special process with emphasis on quality and timesaving techniques. I hope that you will enjoy using these techniques and will be proud of the garments that result. Although this book discusses women's tailoring, you can also use these techniques when making men's garments. Contemporary suits and coats for men have become less rigid and the "hard tailored" look has given way to a more relaxed one. For a "harder" appearance, however, you can substitute a heavier or stiffer interfacing than those required in the instructions in this book.

Note: Consider this book a resource to use with other books containing more information on fabric, pattern alterations, pressing equipment, and more traditional tailoring techniques. Consult the reference list at the end of this book for additional references that I recommend.

TOOLS AND EQUIPMENT

Using quality tools and equipment in the correct manner is as essential to tailoring as selecting the right fabric and pattern. Throughout this book, emphasis is place on precision and accuracy, whether the discussion is about laying out the fabric, cutting, marking, or sewing. Without the proper tools, you will be handicapped in achieving this kind of precision. Assemble the following tools and equipment, before you begin your tailoring project.

PATTERN ADJUSTMENT TOOLS

See-through ruler with grid lines spaced ⅛" (3 mm) apart. Make sure the grid is accurately marked before purchasing.

Fine-tipped marking pens in several colors to mark changes on pattern pieces.

A French curve for help when redrawing necklines and armholes.

TOOLS FOR CUTTING AND MARKING

Dressmaker shears of high quality, hot-forged steel in a solid frame (rather than those with stainless steel blades with plastic handles). This is an investment as well as a necessity when it comes to saving time, work, and stress. An adjustable screw is preferable to a rivet holding the blades together for controlling the tightness of the cutting action.

Shears range from 6" to over 12" in length. The important factor in choosing a pair is fit; two or three fingers should fit into the larger of the rings of the handle and the thumb should fit comfortably snug into the smaller ring. If the thumb ring is too large, your thumb will slip around in it, making it difficult to keep control of the shears. It tires the hand from having to grip the shears more securely and the constant rubbing against the thumb can be painful. Be sure to try out any shears before purchasing and buy the longest one that is within your comfort and price ranges.

Sewing scissors for trimming and clipping seams. These should have very sharp points to get into corners and to do a clean and accurate job of the thinning or grading the seam allowances. A 4"- or 5"-long scissors is the handiest size to keep at the sewing machine.

Tailor's chalk or powdered chalk in a fine-line dispenser for marking. It is best to avoid using waxed chalk on light-colored fabrics as it leaves grease marks when heat is applied.

Darning cotton or embroidery floss for making tailor tacks. The softness and the multiple strands help keep the tacks from accidentally pulling out of the fabric.

PRESSING EQUIPMENT

Proper pressing equipment and techniques go hand in hand with accurate sewing to create a successful tailored garment. Pressing during construction shapes and molds garment pieces, and the final pressing gives the garment a finished look.

The following list includes the pieces of equipment a home sewer should have on hand before beginning a tailoring project. Tailors and dressmakers may have additional pieces of specially designed equipment in their workshops.

Steam iron with a heavy metal sole plate. Most home sewers can make do without the standard professional equipment—flat bed press and pressurized irons—though they are certainly convenient and save much time.

Press cloths. A well-laundered piece of muslin is adequate. See-through and wool press cloths are also available.

Padded pressing board placed on a table or a table padded with an old woolen blanket and then covered with a cotton sheet or cloth gives a firm and stable surface on which to work. The surface should be large enough to hold large garment pieces—large enough so they don't hang over the edge or slip off, as often happens when using a standard ironing board. When applying fusible interfacing, it is necessary to work on a surface that can take pressure and absorb heat and moisture.

Tailor's ham and seam roll. Both should be solidly packed with sawdust and at least one side should be covered with wool. You will use this to support the garment when pressing shaped areas and seams. Keep these within arm's reach on the pressing table.

Point presser made of hard wood. Use this tool to support seams while pressing them open in collars, lapels, and other tight corners. This tool is often referred to as an **edgeboard** in this book.

Clapper. Use this block of hardwood to absorb moisture and heat and set the press after using the steam iron. You can also use it to flatten and take the life and thickness out of bulky seam allowances.

The Tailored Jacket

THE TAILORED JACKET

PATTERN SELECTION

To get the most out of this learning experience, select a jacket pattern that contains the following elements: notched collar and lapels, a center back vent, two-piece sleeves with vents or mock vents, patch pockets, and a full lining (Figure 1). The patch pocket is the easiest design and is integrated in the directions that follow. However, instructions for a variety of other pocket types are included in the jacket chapter and two that are usually found in coats appear in the chapter on coat construction.

back view

Fig 1 front view

Fabric Selection

In a tailored jacket, there are at least three layers of fabric: the fashion or outer fabric, the interfacing, and the lining. Before selecting the fabrics for your tailored jacket, read through the following information.

Fashion Fabric

Although fabric with almost any type of weave and fiber content can be used for a tailored garment, some are much easier to handle and will produce a more successful jacket or coat than others. If you are just getting started with your first tailoring project, choose wool or a wool blend in a fabric that has some texture, a tweed for example. Wool flannel is another possibility but will require a little more careful handling and pressing. Wool is a durable fiber, can be eased and molded with steam from the iron, and it will hold its form once it has been shaped. If you cannot or do not wish to work on wool, consider silk and linen suiting fabrics a good alternative.

Avoid tightly woven, smooth, hard-surfaced fabrics such as worsted flannels, menswear suitings, and gabardine until you have had much more experience with tailoring techniques. Crepe is another weave to save for later, too. It has a tendency to shrink when steam is applied during construction and it is difficult to restore crepe fabric to its original state after over-pressing it.

Purchase fabric of the highest quality you can afford. Economizing on quality affects the overall look of the finished jacket. Regardless of the cost of materials, you will be investing the same amount of time and effort in the project, so why not work on the best?

Lining Fabric

Lining fabric of good quality rayon or acetate are commonly used for tailored garments. Polyester and nylon, though very durable and pliable, do not permit air and moisture to escape through the fibers and are not comfortable to wear. Silk is rich and luxurious, but it is a much weaker fiber than the others listed and more costly. It is not a good lining choice for garments that will receive a lot of wear.

Interfacing

The purpose of interfacing is to give body, stability, strength, and molded shape to the finished garment without adding any obvious bulk. Interfacings are available in the traditional sew-in variety as well as in the newer fusibles. In this book, the focus in the directions for the jacket is on using fusible interfacings. These are available in various weights and can be divided into different categories, determined by their structure.

Interfacing Types

Woven interfacings have a nice hand, drape well, are strong and flexible, and stretch most in the bias direction.

Nonwoven interfacings have a structure similar to paper or felt and are made of fiber webs. If the fibers are laid parallel to each other, the fabric is stable along that grain; in the other direction, it is not as stable and will stretch. If the fibers are placed randomly rather than in a line, the result is an all-bias fabric that stretches in all directions.

Knit interfacings are softer and more supple than woven and nonwoven interfacings and stretch most in the crosswise direction. Fusible knits vary so it is a good idea to do a test fuse on your fashion fabric to determine ahead of time the results you will get in the finished garment.

Weft-insertion interfacings are a cross between a woven and a knit. They have crosswise yarns like a woven fabric, but these are held in place in the lengthwise lines (wales) of warp knitting. This structure combines the softness of knits with stability of wovens. Like wovens, these interfacings have bias give and the lengthwise grain is the most stable.

Note: Fusible interfacing stiffens the area to which it is fused, adding more body than would a sew-in interfacing of comparable weight. It is very important to test-fuse a sample of the selected interfacing on a scrap of your fabric, before making the final decision.

INTERFACING SELECTION

Ideally, interfacing should not dramatically alter the characteristics of the fabric to which it is fused. Smooth fabrics should stay smooth, stretchy ones should retain their stretchability, and soft fabrics should not become overly crisp.

In addition the interfacing you use must be compatible with the fashion fabric when it comes to care and upkeep.

Select a medium-weight weft-insertion or woven interfacing for the body and undercollar of your garment. Choose a lightweight woven, nonwoven or knit fusible interfacing for the upper collar, lapels, and pockets.

FABRIC PREPARATION

Whatever you do, don't skip this step. Adequate preparation before you cut ensures quality results and eliminates unwanted surprises during jacket construction and fitting.

PRETREATING WOOLS AND WOOL BLENDS

Ask a reputable dry cleaner to steam shrink and press your fabric. This is the quickest way to prepare your fabric for cutting and usually quite inexpensive. However, if the fabric is skewed off-grain it may be better to "sheet-treat" your fabric. Another name for this is London shrink. Use this method to correct the grain and preshrink the fabric.

1. Soak a bed sheet in water and wring out to distribute the moisture evenly.
2. Lay the damp sheet on a carpeted floor and place the fabric, folded lengthwise, with selvages matching, in the center of the sheet.
3. Fold the long sides of the sheet over to the center to encase the fabric.
4. Make 12"-deep folds from each end until they meet in the center.
5. Cover with plastic and allow the wool to absorb the moisture for several hours or overnight.
6. Unfold carefully to check the grainline. If the fabric is not square with selvages and crosswise yarns lined up, pull gently on the bias until the fabric is grain perfect.
7. Allow the fabric to dry in place.

LINING FABRIC PREPARATION

Use an iron to press and smooth out any wrinkles in your lining fabric, before cutting the necessary pieces. Most linings tend to lose their original sheen and may water spot if preshrunk. You will learn how to make ample allowances in your lining pattern to compensate for any shrinkage that may occur during construction or in subsequent cleanings.

FUSIBLE INTERFACING PREPARATION

It is important to preshrink all interfacings, even when labeled "preshrunk." Almost all of them will shrink, even after repeated washings. To preshrink fusible interfacing, place them in hot water until saturated with water and then lay flat to dry.

Spraying interfacing with warm water prior to fusing will cause additional shrinkage. You can accomplish the same thing by holding an iron about an inch above the interfacing to steam shrink it prior to fusing. Neither of these methods should replace the initial preshrinking described above. It is important to do this so that any residual shrinkage does not occur while you are fusing; this can cause unsightly bubbles in the fused surface of the fabric.

Choosing and Applying Fusible Interfacing

Interface the "public" layer, the uppermost layer of the garment that shows. This includes the upper collar, the facing side of the lapel, patch pockets, and cuff turnbacks, as well as the garment front. It results in a smooth outer appearance with no hint of seam allowances shadowing through.

Always test-fuse the chosen interfacing on a swatch of the outer fabric before fusing it to the garment. This allows you to evaluate the resulting firmness and to make sure that you are happy with the results.

Jacket Interfacing Weights

Refer to Figure 2.

Select a *medium-weight interfacing* for the following jacket pieces:

1. Jacket front. This interfacing should extend to the armhole and underarm areas. You will also use it in the hem allowance, ending at the hem fold line.
2. Jacket side front. Use in the underarm and hem allowance.
3. Back vent. If your jacket has a back vent, interface the turnback. Also interface the hem allowance.
4. Sleeve. Interface the hem allowance and the vent turnback if the sleeve has this detail.
5. Undercollar. The jacket undercollar is cut on the bias and the interfacing must be cut the same way so that grainlines match.

Choose a *lightweight* fusible interfacing for:
1. Front facing. Interface the lapel area.
2. Upper collar.
3. Patch pocket.

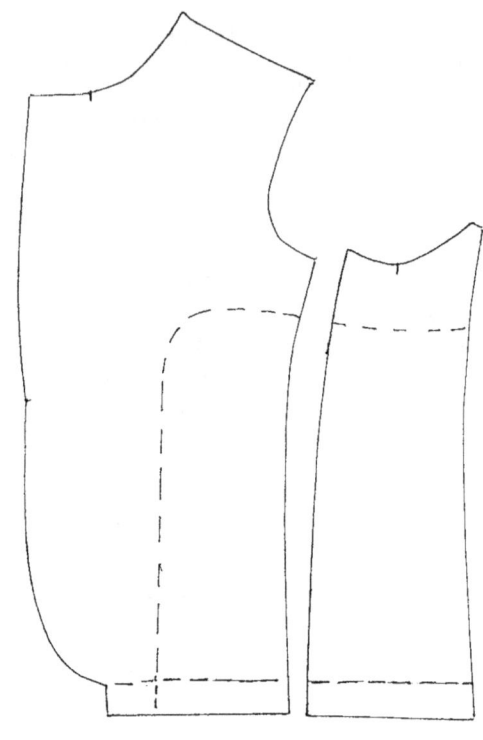

Fig 2   jacket front   side front

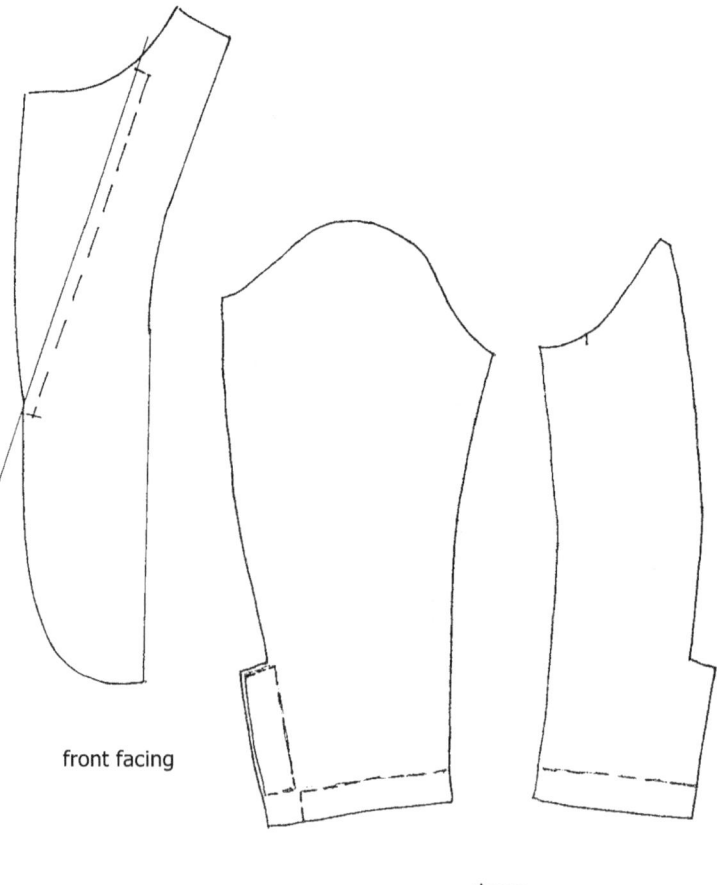

front facing

sleeve

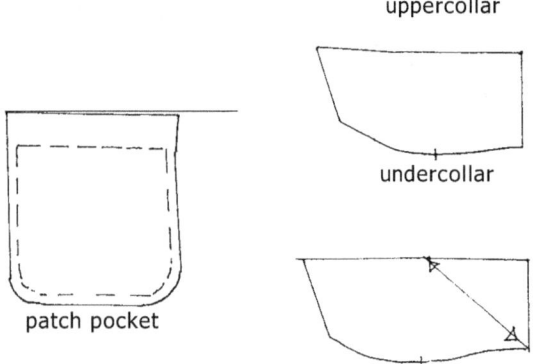

patch pocket

uppercollar

undercollar

HOW TO APPLY FUSIBLE INTERFACING

Successful fusing requires heat, moisture, and very firm pressure using an iron with a metal sole plate. Be sure to read the manufacturer's instructions for fusing. The directions that follow are general and work with most fusible interfacings. However, some of the newer interfacings require a dry iron and/or a lower temperature than that recommended below.

1. Position the interfacing with adhesive side down on the wrong side of the fabric to which it is to be fuse.
2. Cover the interfacing with a press cloth or two layers of white tissue paper. Spray the entire area with a good misting of water.
3. With the iron set for WOOL, position the iron on top of the press cloth and hold in place for about 15 seconds. Apply firm, downward pressure on the iron to ensure a strong fuse.
4. Move the iron to the next location to be fused, being careful not to slide it. The iron should overlap the previously fused area. Fuse as directed above. Repeat this process until all areas have been fused.
5. Smooth the entire area by sliding the iron over the cloth.
6. Allow the fabric to cool before handling.

The illustrations in this book are shaded to make it easy for you to identify the various layers in a tailored garment.

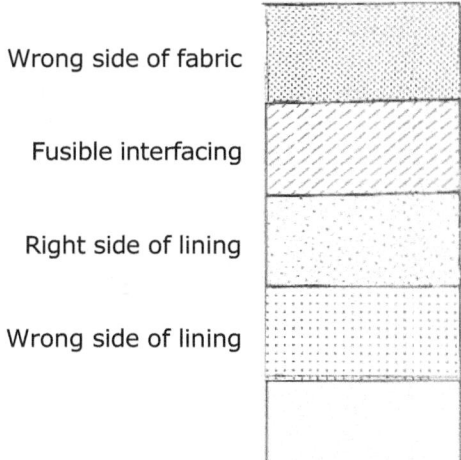

Right side of fabric

Wrong side of fabric

Fusible interfacing

Right side of lining

Wrong side of lining

JACKET PATTERN PREPARATION

Examining a designer's ready-to-wear jacket or blazer reveals some major differences between the pattern and construction methods used by manufacturers and those used by the home sewer. Commercial patterns made for home sewing usually have a uniform ⅝" (1.5cm) seam allowance width throughout. Pattern instructions direct you to stitch this standard seam, then to trim and grade the enclosed seams (collar and facing edges) before turning.

Manufacturers use different seam widths to eliminate the need to trim and clip seams, saving much time and labor. in addition, they may make modifications to certain seams to allow for the roll of the collar and lapel, and to the turn of cloth.

If you are an apparel design student, you must be prepared to handle pattern work in a number of different situations. As in the clothing industry, you must be able to make original patterns from sketches, perfect a knock-off from other garments, and adapt commercial patterns to the manufacturer's needs. In custom work, you must be able to alter and adapt patterns to fit an individual figure.

in this chapter, you will learn:
1. How to adjust seam widths to build in roll where seams must be hidden, such as at the collar, lapel, and front edges.
2. Where and how to allow for the necessary ease in the lining pattern.

Most commercial pattern companies incorporate some ease in their pattern pieces for roll and turn of cloth. The amount and location of the ease is not standard from company to company, so you must remove the ease from the commercial pattern pieces for your jacket before continuing.

To remove the ease:
1. Lay the jacket front facing pattern piece over the jacket front pattern piece and compare the cutting lines of the two along the neckline, lapel, and front edges. If the two are not identical, trace the cutting lines of the jacket front onto the facing pattern piece. Use a colored, fine-line pen to mark this change since all subsequent changes in the seam widths will be made from this new line.

2. Lay the upper collar over the undercollar pattern piece and trace the cutting lines to make the upper collar the same size and shape as the undercollar. However, if the collar style is very narrow, lay the undercollar on top of the upper collar and trace the cutting lines of the upper collar.

3. If there are patch pockets, make the pocket lining the same size as the pocket.

Next, make any pattern alterations that are necessary for your figure. Instructions for making pattern alterations to fit the individual are not covered in this book because there are many excellent resource materials available in various books on alterations, tailoring, and general sewing. Many of these are listed in the Resource list at the end of this book.

You will make the changes described below from the cutting lines, not the seamlines. You will need to make adjustments on the following pattern tissue pieces:
Front
Back
Front Facing
Back Neck Facing
Sleeves
Upper Collar
Undercollar

Patch Pockets (if your pattern has this design feature)

Note: Many European patterns have only the stitching lines marked and *you must add the appropriate seam allowances.* Remember that the directions for the pattern adjustments that follow all relate to the cutting line, not the stitching line.

JACKET FRONT

On the neckline from the shoulder seam around the lapel and down the front to the break point (the bottom of the roll line), make the seam width ⅜" (1 cm) wide by removing ¼" (6mm) from the existing seam allowance.

2. On the lower front edge from the break point down around the curve, make the seam width ½" (1.3 cm) by trimming ⅛" (3 mm) from the seam allowance.
(Figure 3).

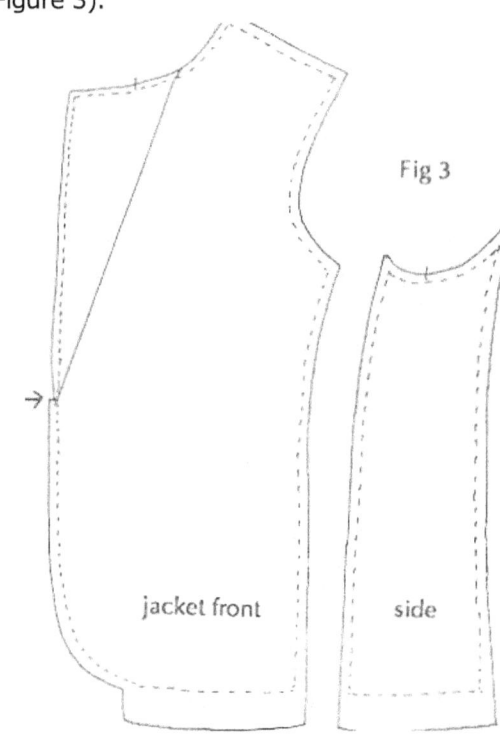

Fig 3

break point →

jacket front   side

Note: As a result of these two changes, there will be definite jog at the break point where the seam widths change from ⅜" to ½". *Do not blend the widths*

3. The usual hem allowance on commercial patterns is either 1 ⅝" (4 cm) or 2" (5 cm). No change is required.

4. If the lapel roll line is not marked on the pattern, extend the shoulder seamline into the neck area (from the point where the stitching lines of the shoulder and neckline intersect) 1" (2.5cm) for women's jackets and 1 ¼" (3.2 cm) for men's jackets. Draw a straight line from that point to the break point of the lapel *at the stitching line,*

not the cutting line (Figure 4).

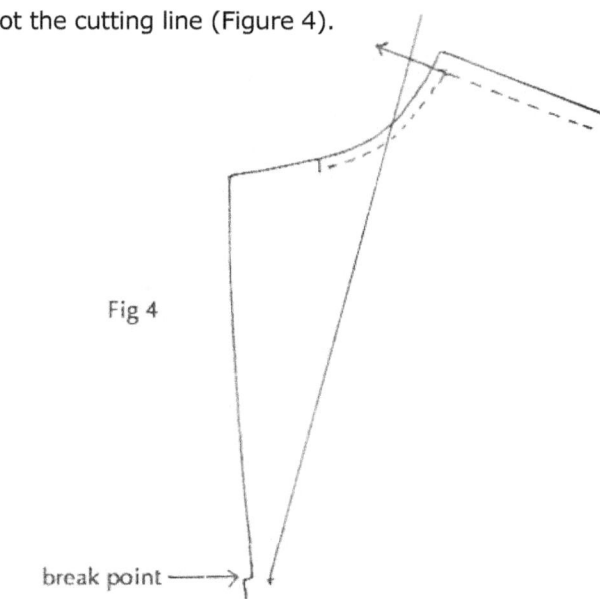

Fig 4

break point →

JACKET BACK

1. On the neckline seam, change the seam width to ⅜" (1 cm) by removing ¼" (6mm) from the seam allowance (Figure 5).

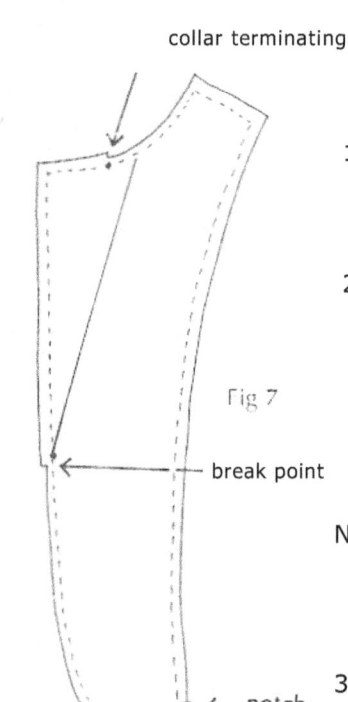

Fig 5
jacket back

2. Check the center back vent (if the pattern has one) to make sure it is the desired length. A back vent usually opens to the waist.

If you wish to add a vent, add 2 ⅝" (6.7 cm) from the center back seam, beginning ⅝" (1.5cm) above the waistline and extending it to the hem (figure 6)

In some patterns, the back vent hem corner has been cut away. If this is so in the pattern you are using, fill in the area to correspond with the vent requirements given above.

3. The back hem allowance should be the same width as the front hem allowance.

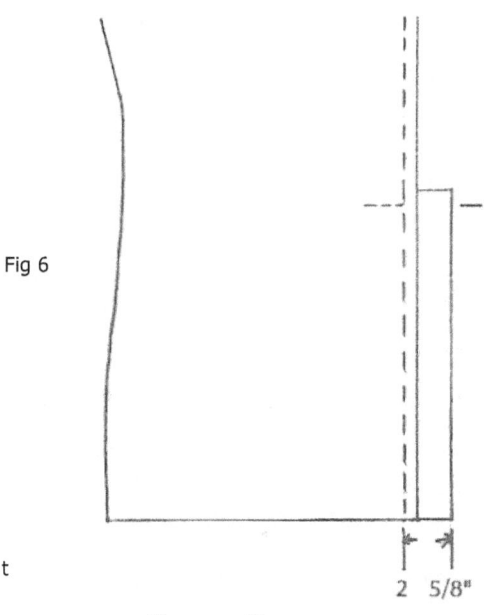

Fig 6

2 5/8"

FRONT FACING

1. Reduce the seam width of the neckline to ⅜" (1 cm) starting at the shoulder seam and ending at the collar termination point by trimming ¼" (6 mm) from the pattern tissue.

2. Change the seam width to ½" (1.3 cm) on the lapel area from the collar termination point around and down to the break point of the lapel by trimming ⅛" (3mm) from the pattern tissue. From the break point down and around the front curve, change the seam width to ⅜" (1 cm) by trimming ¼" (6 mm) from the seam allowance.

Note: There will be a jog in two places along this line, one at the collar termination point, the other at the break point of the lapel. *Do not blend the seam widths.*

3. Transfer the lapel roll line from the jacket front to the facing pattern piece (Figure 7).

4. Mark the notch about 1 ½" (3.8 cm) from the bottom of the inner edge of the front facing, the edge that will be stitched to the front lining.
5. If the grainline on the pattern is parallel to the lower center front line, consider changing it so that the grainline is parallel to the outside edge of the lapel. This will make the lapel look more attractive.

BACK NECK FACING

Reduce the seam width at the neckline to ⅜" (1cm) by trimming away ¼" (6 mm).

SLEEVES

1. If there is no vent at the wrist, and you would like one, add an extension of 1 ½" (3.8 cm) to the outside (elbow) seam of both the upper and under sleeve pattern pieces.
2. If there is a sleeve vent on the pattern pieces already, but different from the one illustrated here, change it to match the illustrations here (Figure 8).
3. The hem allowances should be the same as those on the jacket front and back pattern pieces.

COLLAR

1. Make sure that the cutting lines on the upper and under collar are identical before making the following adjustments.
2. Trim the seam width of the undercollar to ⅜" (1 cm) all around (Figure 9).
3. Reduce the seam width of the upper collar to ½" (1.3 cm) all around (Figure 10).

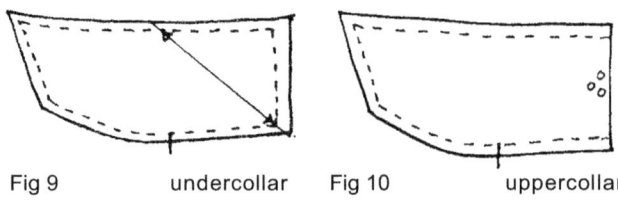

Fig 9   undercollar   Fig 10   uppercollar

PATCH POCKET

1. If the pocket pattern has square corners, curve the bottom corners. Patch pockets with curved corners are much easier to construct and apply to the jacket than those with squared corners.
2. Check the hem allowance at the upper edge. It should be 1 ¼" (3.2 cm).
3. Adjust the seam allowance width to ½" (1.3 cm) all the way around, excluding the hem edge (Figure 11).

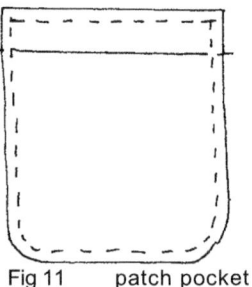

Fig 11   patch pocket

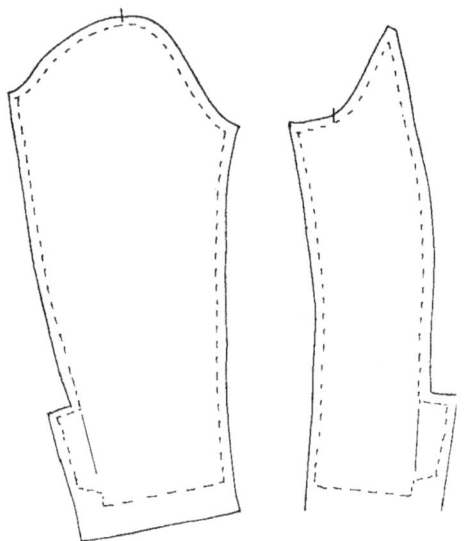

Fig 8 upper sleeve under sleeve

Lining Pattern Preparation

The jacket lining hides the inner construction of the completed jacket and protects it from wear. It also makes it easier to slip the jacket on and off. To allow for the necessary ease in the finished jacket, the lining pattern requires some special adjustments.

Front Lining

Refer to Figures 12 and 13.

1. Allow a 1"-deep (2.5 cm) pleat in the shoulder seam (if not already existing in the lining pattern) for bustline ease. To do this, tape a piece of tissue paper under the front lining pattern piece from the shoulder to the bustline. Extend the shoulder seam toward the center front 1" (2.5 cm) and connect to a point at the bust level along the front edge of the lining pattern piece.
2. Draw in a 1"- deep pleat from the center of the shoulder. Fold out the pleat and draw a straight line across the shoulder cutting line. (When you cut on the line and open the pattern, a peak will form at the shoulder edge).
3. Before cutting, add 1/8" (3 mm) beyond the shoulder cutting line for a total shoulder seam width of 3/4" (2 cm). Cut on the new cutting line.
4. Add 1/8" (3 mm) beyond the outer edge of the shoulder and taper this into the underarm cutting line, using a French Curve.
5. When the front lining pattern is laid over the jacket front pattern, you will find the lining to be 3/4" (2 cm) shorter than the jacket when the hem allowance is 1 5/8" (4 cm). The lining will be 1" (2.5 cm) shorter when there is a 2" (5 cm) hem allowance designated on the pattern.
6. Line up the inner edge of the front facing pattern with the front edge of the front lining pattern and mark a notch matching the one on front facing near the lining hemline.

Back Lining

Refer to Figure 14.

1. Place the back lining pattern over the jacket back pattern piece and trace the jacket stitching and cutting lines onto the lining pattern if the two are not alike in size. If the pattern has a back vent, include the vent in the tracing. If the pattern has a back vent, complete steps 2, and 3 and then proceed to the box on page 21.

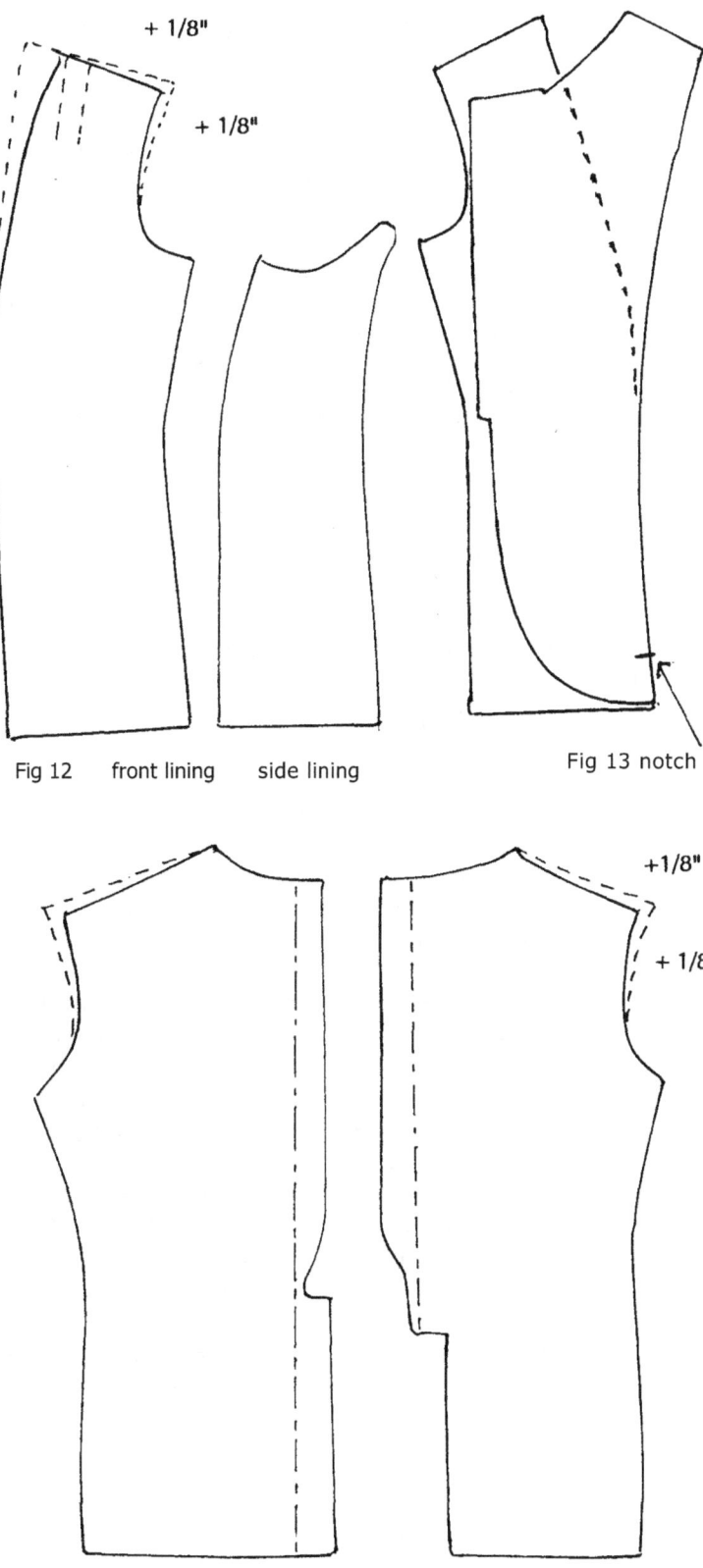

Fig 12   front lining   side lining   Fig 13 notch

back lining right side (turn back side

Fig 14 back lining left side (underlap side)

2. Add ⅛" (3 mm) to the shoulder and armhole edge at the shoulder, tapering at the underarm curve as you did for the front lining.

Note: For a jacket without a vent, check the lining pattern for a 1" - deep (2.5 cm) pleat, extending from the center back line.

3. Replace the back lining pattern piece on top of the jacket back pattern piece and adjust if necessary so that the lining pattern is ¾" (2 cm) shorter than the jacket pattern if the jacket hem allowance is 1 ⅝" (4 cm). If the jacket hem allowance is 2" (5 cm), cut the lining pattern 1" shorter than the jacket back pattern piece.

BACK LINING IF YOU ADDED A VENT

Refer to Figures 15 and 16

1. Place a large piece of tissue paper over the jacket back pattern piece and trace the jacket stitching and cutting lines. Include the added vent in the tracing.
2. Complete steps 2 and 3, above, before proceeding. To be safe, make right and left back lining patterns and with the pattern pieces lying face up, label them right back and left back lining.
3. On both the left and right back lining pieces, add 1" (2.5cm) beyond the center back cutting line for a pleat, tapering back to the original cutting line just above the vent.
4. On the right back lining piece, fold under the vent extension along the fold line (an extension of the center back line). Trace along the edges of the vent extension on the pattern tissue as indicated by the dashed lines in Figure 15.

For the new cutting line, draw a line parallel to and 1 ¼" (3 cm) from both dashed lines. Next, extend the cutting line above the vent to meet the new cutting line. Cut away the excess pattern on the new cutting lines (the shaded section of the right back lining in Figure 16).

5. Allow for a ⅝"-wide (1.5 cm) seam allowance at the back neckline. You will sew this seam, however, with a ⅜"-wide (1 cm) seam allowance to give ¼" (6 mm) ease in the length above the vent. This prevents pulling at the top of the vent.

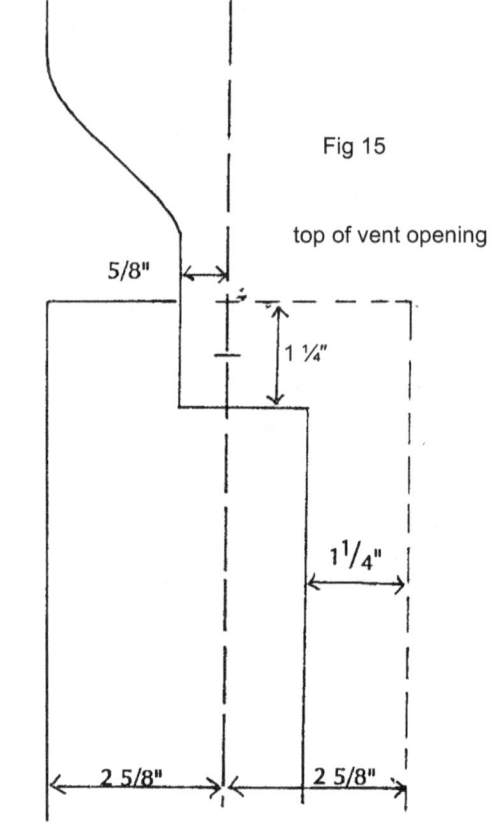

Fig 15

top of vent opening

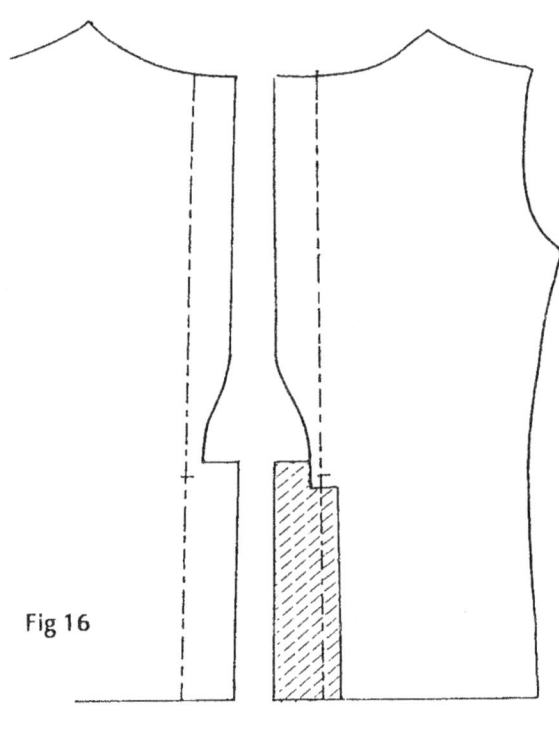

Fig 16

left, underlap side   right, turn back side

Sleeve Lining

Refer to Figure 17.

1. If the sleeve pattern has a vent, omit it on the sleeve lining pattern pieces (if not already done).
2. Cut the sleeve lining pattern pieces ¾" (2 cm) shorter than the sleeve pattern pieces if the hem allowance is 1 ⅝" (4 cm) and 1" (2.5 cm) if the hem allowance is 2" (5 cm).
3. Raise the sleeve cap ¼" (6 mm) at the shoulder, tapering to nothing as shown at the seams of the upper sleeve.
4. Raise the underarm ¼" (6 mm) and taper to nothing at the seams.

Patch Pocket Lining

Change the seam allowance on the lining pattern to ⅜" (1 cm) all around except at the top edge, which should be cut even with the top edge of the finished pocket.

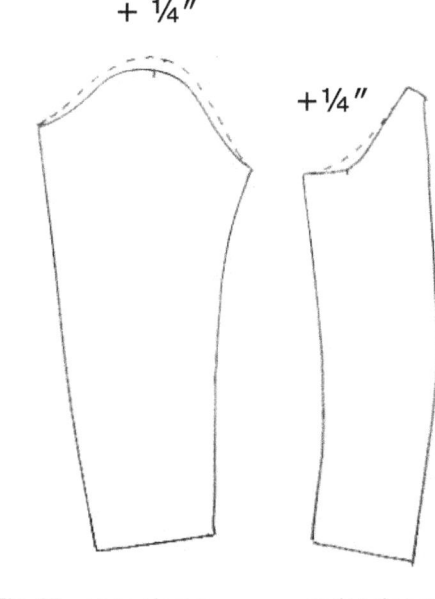

Fig 17 upper sleeve   under sleeve

Interfacing Pattern Preparation

Commercial patterns may or may not include separate pattern pieces for the interfacing. If not, it is easy to create your own using the facing and garment pattern pieces. Even if they are included, they may require some adjustments for better support in the finished garment. Prepare pattern pieces for interfacing in the following manner.

Front

1. Use the adjusted front facing pattern to draft a front interfacing pattern piece. Place the facing pattern piece on top of the jacket front pattern piece.
2. Extend the upper portion of the interfacing pattern all the way over to the armhole and down 3" (7.5 cm) from the underarm curve of the jacket (Figure 18).
3. Extend the cutting line in the lower half of the facing to make the inner edge of the interfacing 1" wider than the original facing (or if there is a dart, extend the inner edge of the facing all the way to the stitching line of the dart).
4. If there is a side section, mark the underarm interfacing shape 3" below the underarm and draw in a gently curving line as shown in Figure 18.

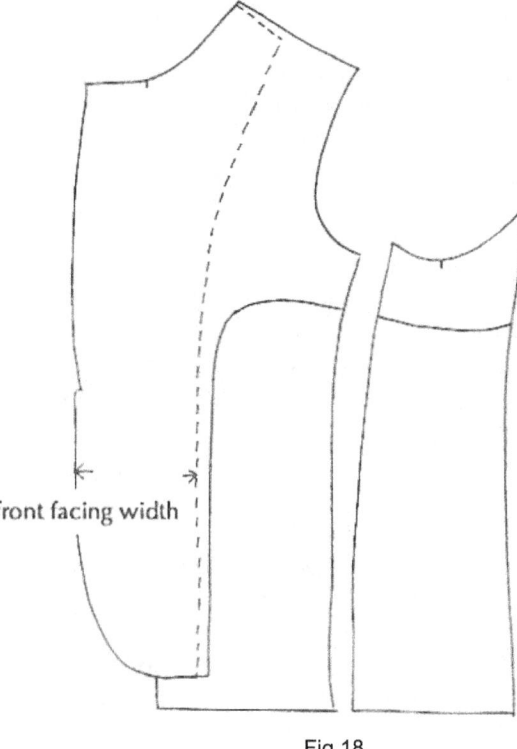

Fig 18

5. Trace the new front and underarm interfacing patterns onto separate pieces of tissue paper.

FRONT FACING

1. Trace the upper half of the facing onto pattern tissue paper.
2. Extend the lapel area ¾" (2 cm) past the roll line toward the inner edge of the facing and draw a line parallel to the roll line. Cut the interfacing pattern apart on this drawn line (Figure 19).

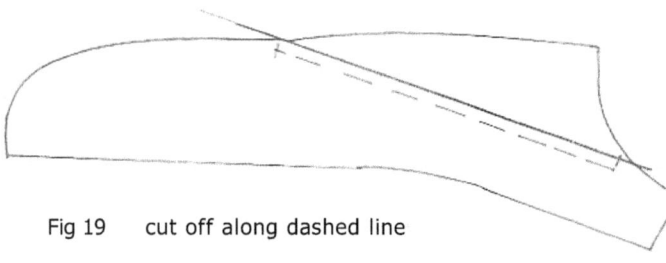

Fig 19   cut off along dashed line

PATCH POCKET

1. Trace the cutting lines of the pocket pattern onto pattern tissue.
2. Remove ⅜" (1 cm) around the outer edge of the traced pattern piece. (There should be no seam allowances on the pocket interfacing.)

HEMS

Interface all hem allowances on the front, side front section, back, and upper and under sleeve pieces. To do so, cut hem interfacing strips on the crosswise grain in the same width as the hem depths on the jacket pattern pieces (either 1 ⅝" (4 cm) or 2" (5 cm).

VENTS

1. To interface the back vent, cut the interfacing the same width and length as the vent from the center back to the outer edge. Cut only 1 vent interfacing. Interface only the vent portion that turns to the inside along the center back fold.
2. Cut narrow strips of interfacing for the portion of each sleeve vent that turns to the inside.

COLLARS

1. Use the adjusted undercollar pattern piece to cut the interfacing.
2. Use the adjusted upper collar pattern piece cut the interfacing.

CUTTING AND PREPARING TO SEW THE JACKET

Ready-to-wear tailoring methods require precise cutting and accurate marking. Follow the steps below to ensure an accurately cut garment.

CUTTING THE JACKET AND LINING PIECES

1. Place the fabric on the cutting table in a single layer or folded in half lengthwise with selveges even and close to you. if the fabric is folded, run a yardstick between the layers to remove bubbles and creases and to separate the layers that stick together.

Note: If your fabric is a stripe or plaid you will need to take care in laying out each piece so the design lines match. It is best to cut the garment pieces from a single layer of fabric to facilitate matching.

2. Position the pattern pieces on the fabric, paying careful attention to grainline; pin or weight in place.
3. Chalk mark carefully around each pattern piece. Make sure that you have placed and marked all garment pieces before you begin to cut.
4. Cut carefully along the chalked lines, using the full length of the blades of sharp dressmaker's shears. Avoid using only the tips. Long strokes produce smoother cut edges than do short choppy strokes. It is easier to stitch accurate seams if the edges of the pieces are smoothly cut.

CUTTING AND APPLYING THE INTERFACING PIECES

How you position the interfacing pattern pieces on the fusible interfacing depends on the type of interfacing you are using.

If you are using a *woven fusible* interfacing, place each pattern piece on the same grainline as that of the area it will interface.

No special layout is required if you are using a *nonwoven, all-bias fusible* interfacing.

For a *nonwoven or knit interfacing with directional give* (usually more stretch in the crosswise direction), follow the same guidelines as you would for a woven interfacing.

- When using weft-insertion fusible interfacing, lay out the pieces as you would for a woven interfacing.

Cut the interfacing pieces, carefully, just as you do the jacket pieces to ensure accuracy. Then fuse the interfacing to all pertinent garment pieces, referring to "How to Apply Fusible Interfacing" on page 15. Figure 20 shows all interfacing fused in place in the correct locations.

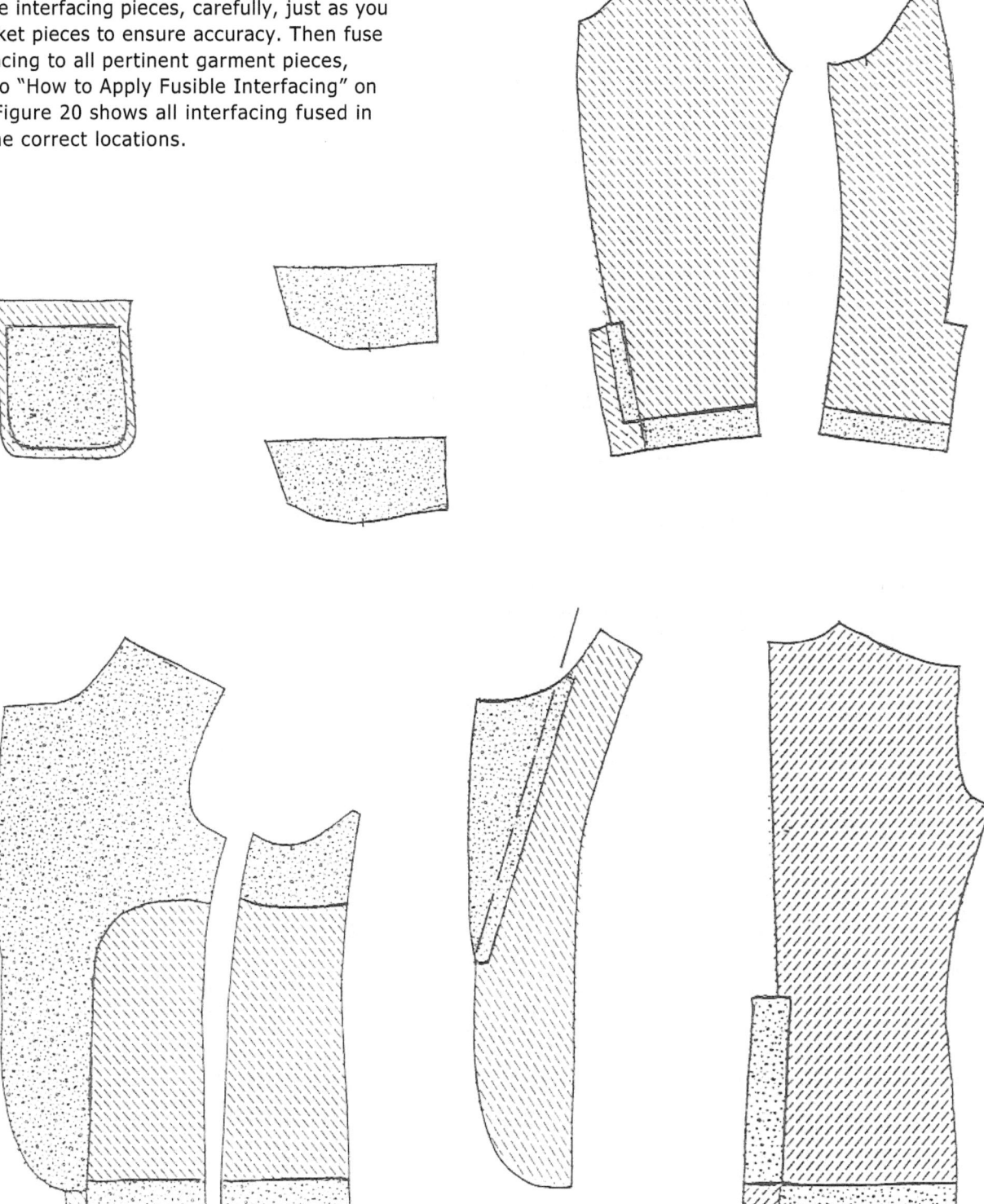

Fig 20

Fig 21

MARKING

1. Replace the appropriate pattern piece on each interfaced garment piece and re-cut if the fabric stretched out of shape during the bonding.
2. Mark the following with tailor tacks or mark stitches. See directions for these on page 53. Figure 21 shows the locations for mark stitches, designated with circles.

    Dart points
    Collar termination point on the front and front facing necklines
    Pocket location
    Underarm points on the side front and under sleeve
    Shoulder location on the neckline edge of the upper and under collar pieces
    Shoulder point on upper sleeve cap

3. Mark the following locations with $3/16"$ (5 mm) clips in the seam allowances, shown in Figure 21 with short, straight lines:

    Front facing and front lining about 1½" (3.8 cm) above the hems; look for notches you marked on the pattern pieces
    Shoulder point on the sleeve cap of the garment and lining pieces
    Dart legs where they end at the seam edge
    Shoulder pleat leg
    Fold line for hem on patch pocket

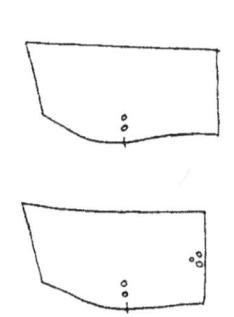
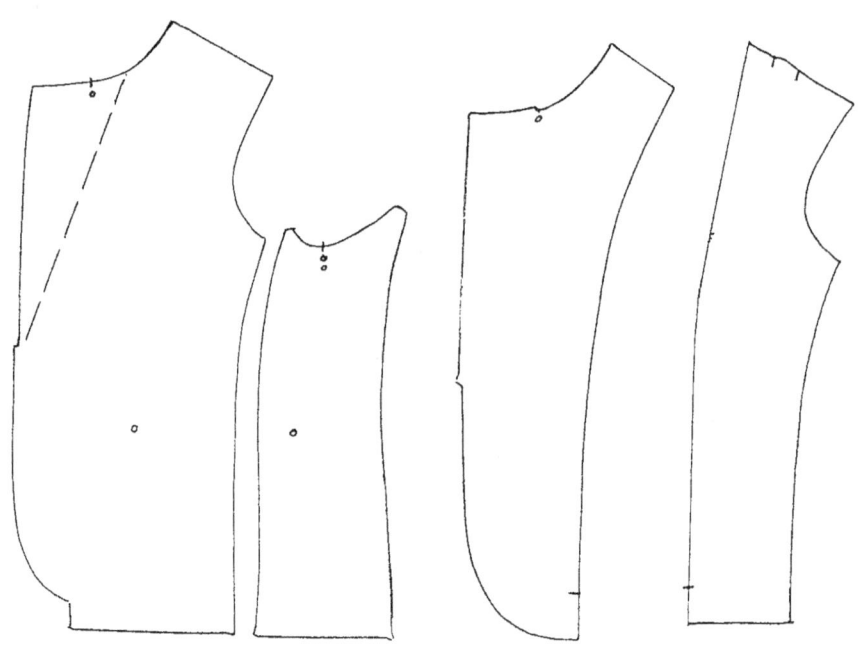

4. Chalk mark the roll line on the interfacing side of the jacket fronts. Chalk in another line parallel to the roll line ¼" (6 mm) toward the armhole.
5. Cut a narrow strip of paper-backed fusible web, fuse it to a piece of ⅜"-wide (1 cm) cotton or linen edge tape. Remove the backing paper. Place the edge of the edge tape ¼" (6 mm) away from the roll line, using the chalk line just drawn as a guide. Fuse to the garment with just a little ease in the garment (up to ½"), thereby shortening the roll line so the jacket will fit more snugly in the chest area without gapping (Figure 22).

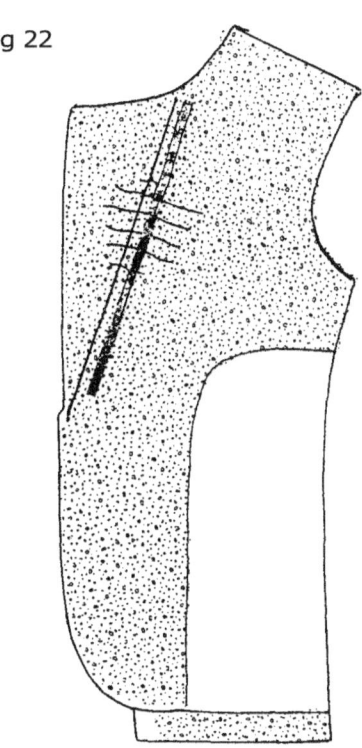

Fig 22

Note: Edge tape is a ⅜"-wide cotton or linen tape used by tailors to stabilize seams and edges to keep garment parts from stretching. Fabric stores most often carry the tape in ¼" (6 mm) or ½" (1.3 cm) widths. The ⅜" width can be purchased from tailoring supply houses. Two sources are listed on page 78. Most recently, fusible edge tape has also been made available. If that is what you are using, there is no need to add a strip of fusible web to the tape before fusing it to the jacket. In a pinch, I have used the selveges from cotton broadcloth or muslin, cut ⅜" (6 mm) wide, when I have run out of edge tape.

JACKET AND LINING CONSTRUCTION

The order of sewing that follows is designed to speed construction by grouping work into time- and energy-saving units that minimize hand work.

PREPARING FOR STITCHING

First pin and then stitch all seams and darts in the lining and jacket as listed below. There is no need to cut the thread after each piece is stitched. To save time, simply chain sew by feeding each piece under the foot without lifting it or cutting the thread between pieces. *Stitch all seams using a ⅝" wide (1.5 cm) seam allowance unless otherwise directed.*

1. Pin the following seams and darts in the *lining*
   Darts and tucks in the front and back (if in your pattern)
   Side panel to the front
   Jacket front facing to the front lining down to the notches near the hem (Figure 23)

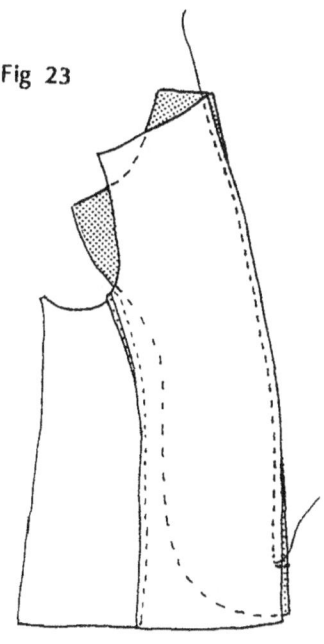

Fig 23

Center back seam from the neckline to the top of the vent if there is one (Figure 24), or to the bottom edge if there is no vent
Upper sleeve to under sleeve along the outseam (Figure 25)
Patch pocket lining to the top edge of the pocket (Figure 26).

2. Pin the following seams and darts in the *jacket pieces:*

   All darts
   Side panel to the front
   Center back seam from the neckline to the top of the vent if there is one, or to the bottom edge if there is no vent (Figure 27)
   Upper sleeve to under sleeve along the outseam (Figure 28)

   Undercollar center back seam (Figure 29).

Fig 24

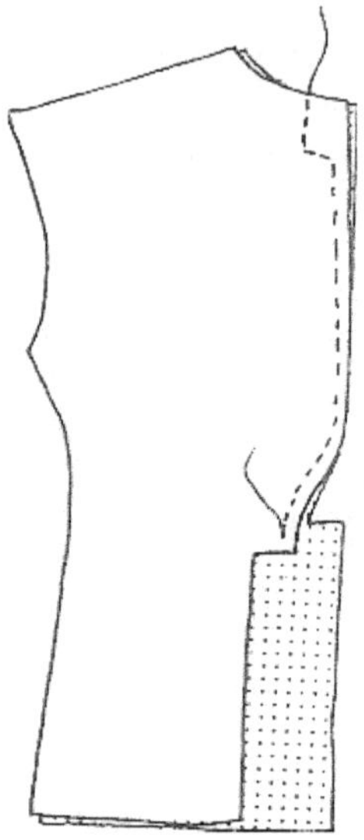

Fig 25

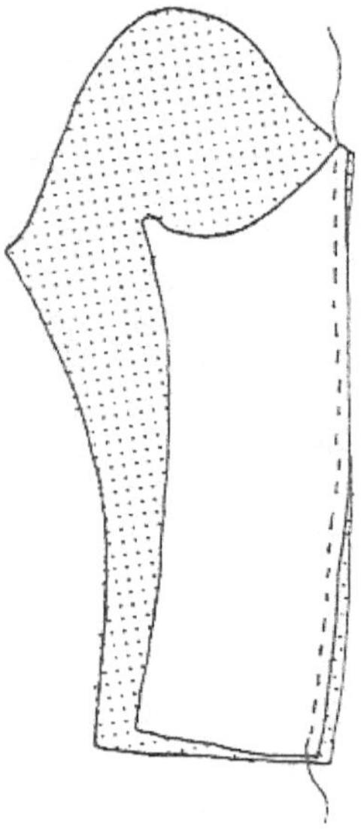

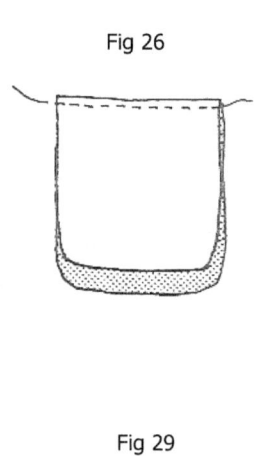

Fig 26

Fig 27

Fig 28

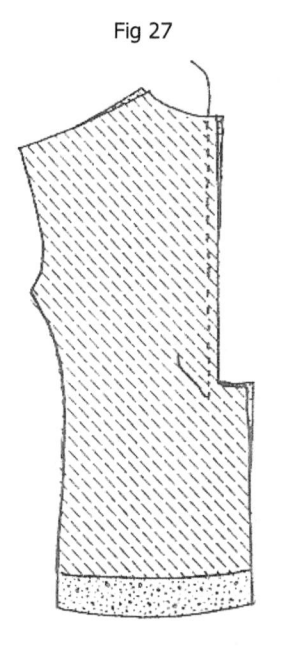

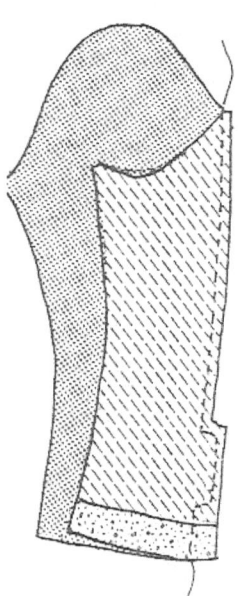

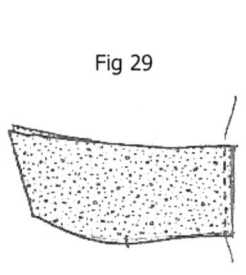

Fig 29

Pressing

After chain stitching all darts and seams, cut the thread chain that formed between the pieces. Take them all to the pressing area and press as directed below.

1. Lightly press all vertical darts and tucks in the *lining* toward the center front or center back.
2. Press the front lining/facing seam toward the lining; the pressed crease should be in the lining fabric along the seam edge, not in the jacket fabric (facing).
3. In the jacket, slash darts through the center as far as possible to reduce bulk and press them open.
4. Press all seams open in the jacket (undercollar, center back, side front, and sleeve seams). Leave the seams in the lining unpressed until you are ready to do a final press of the completed garment. Then press the seam allowances toward the center front or center back and if lining is too loose in any location, you can adjust the lining fit by pressing a tuck or pleat along the seamline as you press it in the desired direction.

Note: If the jacket has a back neck facing, sew the back neckline of the lining to the facing and press the seam toward the lining. It may be necessary to clip into the seam of the lining to make the seam lie flat.

Patch Pocket Assembly

1. Fold the lining over the pocket at the hem fold line and mark balance lines around the bottom curves. Since the lining was cut slightly smaller than the pocket, a bit of the pocket fabric will extend all around the outer edge of the lining as shown (Figure 30).
2. Pin the pocket to the lining, matching the marks and *lining up the cut edges of the pocket and the lining.* Stitch around the outer edge of the pocket, using a ⅜"-wide (1 cm) seam allowance. Ease in the fullness at the curves and leave about 2" (5 cm) open at the bottom edge for turning (Figure 31).
3. Press the seam allowance back toward the pocket, not toward the lining (Figure 34).
4. Turn the pocket right side out through the opening left along the bottom edge and press from the lining side. The pocket fabric should roll to the lining side since the lining is slightly smaller.

Collar Assembly

Before sewing the upper collar to the undercollar, determine which edge is the neckline edge by locating the notches that correspond to the jacket shoulder seam (Figure 33). Collar styles vary in size and shape so it is very important to do this before proceeding. A standard shape is illustrated, but your collar may look different.

1. Pin the outer edges of the undercollar to the upper collar with right sides together. Since the upper collar is slightly larger than the undercollar, there will be a slight amount of ease in the upper collar near the collar points.
2. Stitch the collars together, using a ⅜"-wide (1 cm) seam and leaving ⅜" (1 cm) unstitched at the neckline edge on both halves of the collar (Figure 34).
3. Press the seam open over a point presser.
4. Trim the seam allowance of the upper collar to $^{3}/_{16}$" (5 mm), or less if the fabric will not ravel. The fused interfacing helps stabilize the edges so it is safe to trim this closely.

Note: Trimming the upper collar rather than the undercollar is a departure from the standard method of trimming recommended in most books and pattern guide sheets. With this method, the seam allowances inside the enclosed seam are not doubled over at the turned edge, which often happens with the traditional trimming method, creating an unsightly ridge at the outer edge.

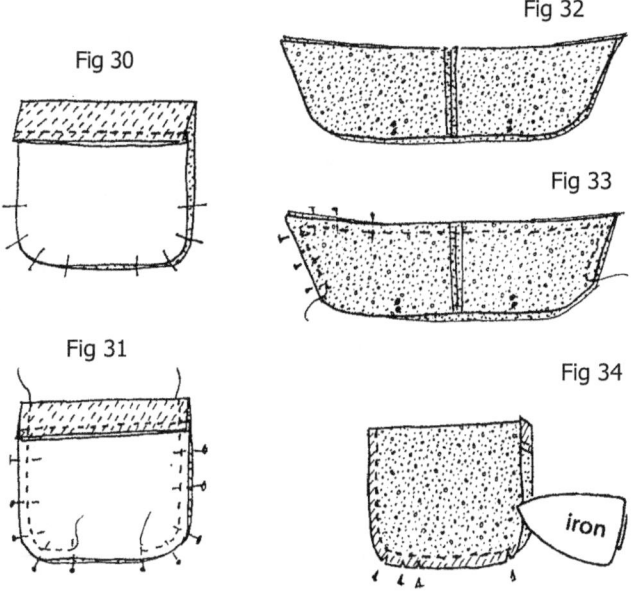

Fig 30

Fig 31

Fig 32

Fig 33

Fig 34

5. Turn the collar right side out and press the edges. The upper collar should roll to the under collar side since the upper collar was cut slightly larger than the undercollar.

SLEEVE ASSEMBLY (WITH MOCK VENTS)

The instructions that follow are for a sleeve designed with a mock vent. This is the method manufacturers often use to cut costs. If you prefer traditional vents in two-piece jacket sleeves, see "Sleeves with Vents," on the next page.

1. Attach the sleeve lining to the sleeve at the hem edge with a ⅝"-wide (1 cm) seam (Figure 35).
2. Keeping the right sides of the sleeve and lining together, bring the lining up to the top edge of the jacket sleeve, forcing the hem to turn up. (Remember the sleeve lining was cut shorter than the jacket sleeve.) Fold the hem at the fold line. There will be tuck in the lining where the two are joined (Figure 36).
3. Pin the lining tuck to the hem of the sleeve on each side.
4. Open out the sleeve and lining and pin the underarm seam edges together as shown. Stitch, using a ⅝"-wide (1.5 cm) seam allowance (Figure 37). Press the seam open.
5. Turn up sleeve hem and tack hem to seams where possible. Set sleeves aside.

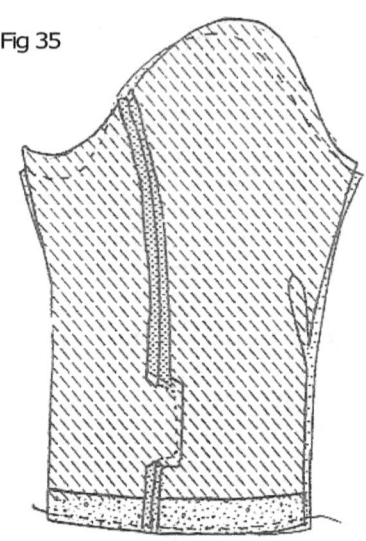

Fig 35

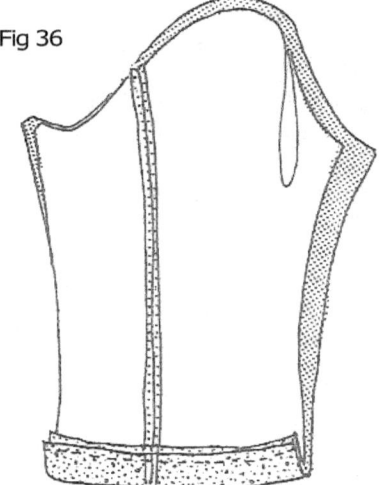

Fig 36

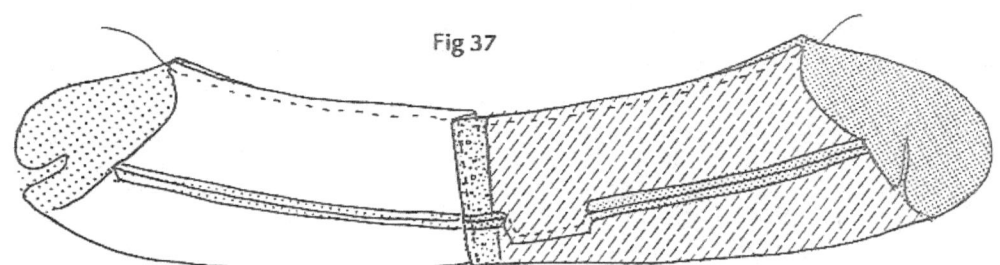

Fig 37

Sleeves with Vents

1. Pin and stitch the upper sleeve to the under sleeve along the outseam to the top of the vent (Figure 38).
2. Press the seam open to the top of the vent, creasing the vent fold-back at the fold line. Turn the hem allowance into its finished position and mark the points where the hem and the vent edges meet (Figure 39).
3. Open the vent corner and chalk mark a line connecting the two marks (Figure 40).
4. With right sides together, pin at the two marks and stitch on the chalked line (Figure 41). *Do not trim this mitered seam.*
5. Press the seam open and distributing the fabric evenly to each side of the seam, press lightly along the originally creased lines.
6. Clip into the corner at the top of the vent on the underlap side (Figure 42). With right sides together, fold the hem allowance up and adjust the length so that the underlap is about ⅛" shorter than the mitered side of the hem. Stitch using a ¼"-wide seam allowance (Figure 43).
7. Turn the hem of the underlap to the outside and with cut edges together, stitch the underlap to the mitered turnback in a ¼"-wide seam allowance (Figure 44).
8. Follow the directions for the mock vent sleeves, beginning with step 1. When attaching the sleeve lining to the completed traditional vent, it is necessary to break it into two steps, breaking the stitching when you reach the vent (Figure 45).

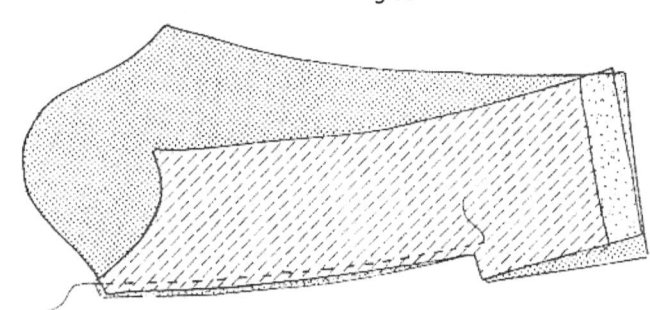
Fig 38

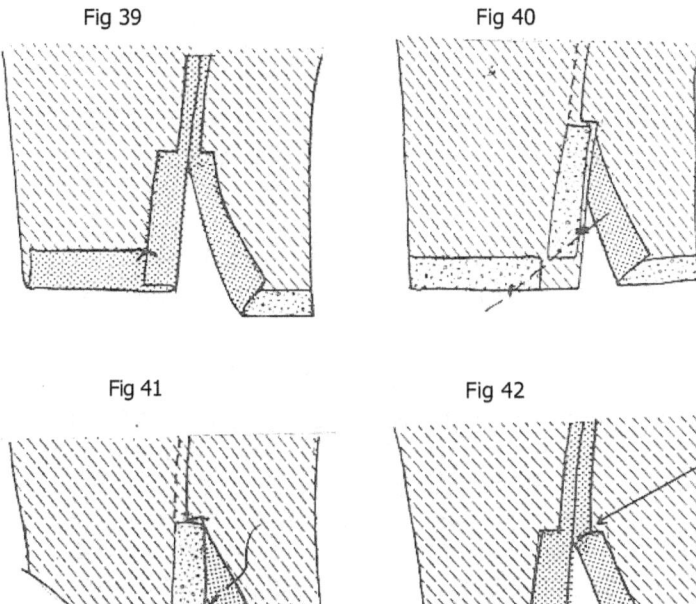
Fig 39 Fig 40

Fig 41 Fig 42

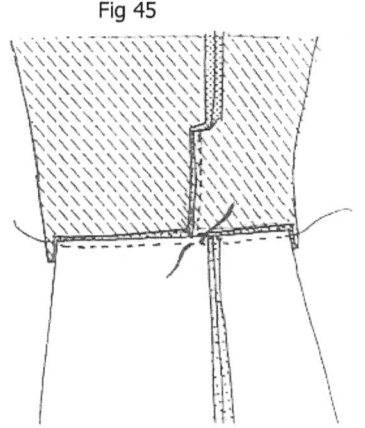
Fig 45

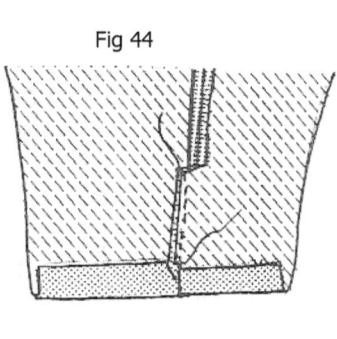
Fig 44

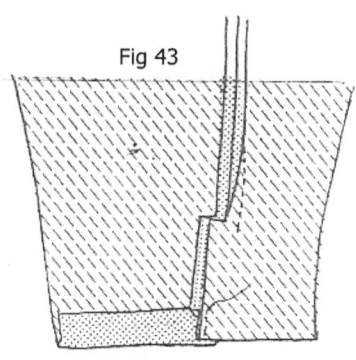
Fig 43

Pocket Application

If your jacket has patch pockets apply them to the jacket front now. If your jacket has another pocket style such as welt or flap pockets, see the special chapter on pockets, beginning on page 38. The method for applying the pockets given below is standard. See page 42, if you prefer to try an "Inside Stitched Patch Pocket."

To apply patch pockets:
1. Position each pocket on a jacket front at the pocket placement marks. Work over a pressing ham to simulate the curvature of the body.
2. Pin the pocket in place. By working over the ham, you will create a bit of ease in the pocket so it curves around your body when you put the jacket on.
3. Topstitch or edgestitch the pocket in place (Figure 46).

Center Back Vent

1. If you have not yet applied interfacing to the jacket back hem allowances and vent turnback, do so now. See page 19.
2. Miter the corner of the turn back at the hem, referring to the steps illustrated in Figure 47. Press the mitered seam open, but do not trim. It may be necessary to adjust the mitered corner ⅛" to 3/16" (3 to 6 mm) later as it must be slightly longer than the vent underlap.

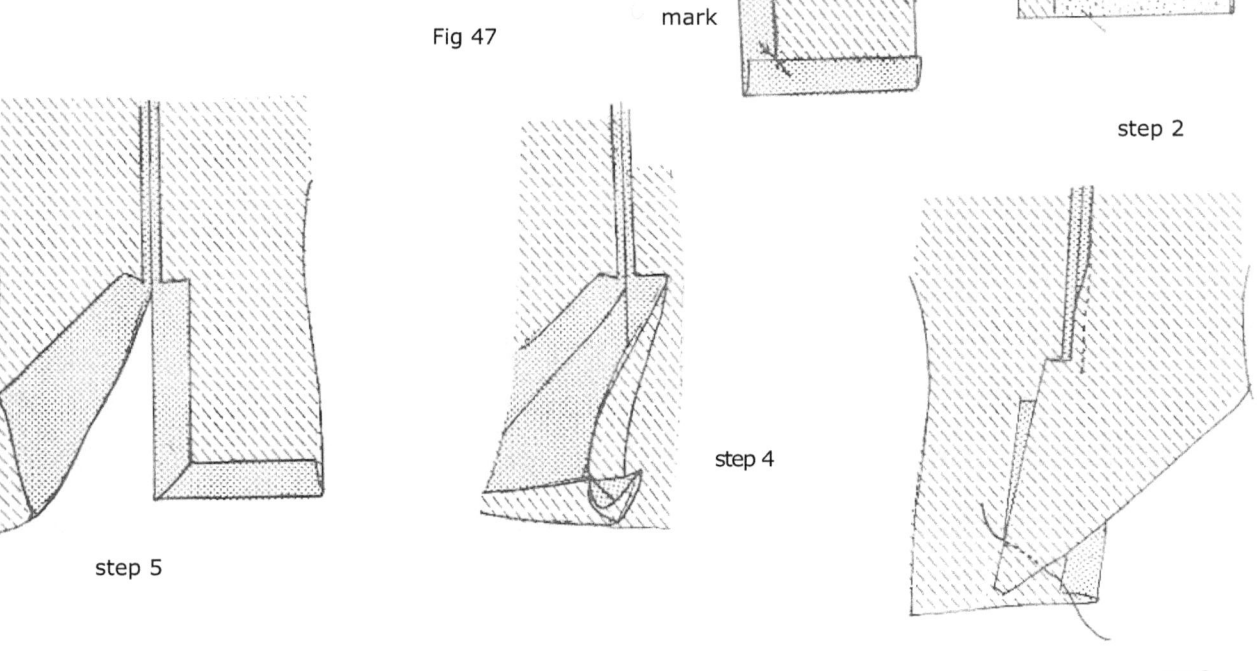

Fig 46 — Edge Stitched, Top Stitched, Double Top Stitched

Fig 47 — step 1, mark, step 2, step3, step 4, step 5

3. With right sides together, stitch the hems of the jacket and the lining together on the underlap side of the vent. Leave about 2" (5cm) unstitched at the side seam. Pin the lining to the jacket at the top of the vent opening, then turn up the jacket hem as shown and adjust the length of the underlap so that it does not hang below the vent turnback (Figure 48).
4. Stitch through all layers from the top of the underlap to the bottom edge of the hem (Figure 49).

    Turn underlap right side out and press.
5. At the top of the vent, clip diagonally into the seam allowance of the lining and the jacket *on the underlap side only* (Figure 50).
6. Pin the completed underlap to the vent turnback in its finished position (Figure 51).

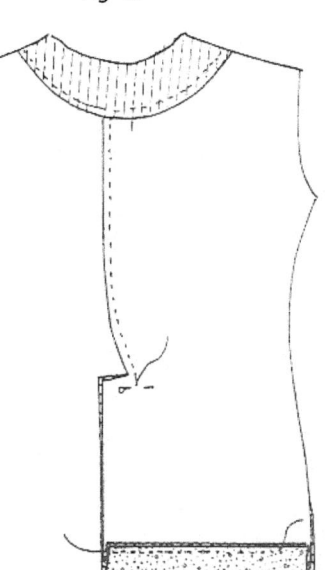

Fig 48

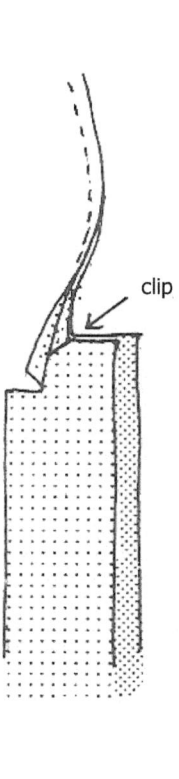

Fig 50

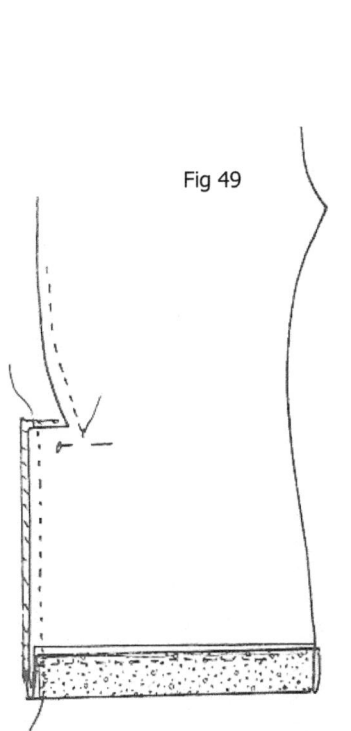

Fig 49

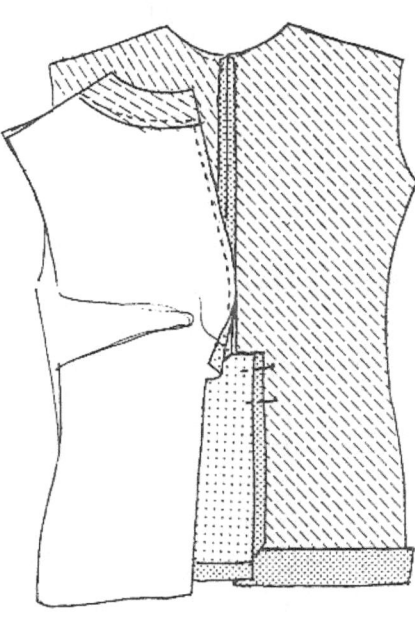

Fig 51

7. Turn down the upper half of the lining (neck and shoulder area) to expose the seam at the top of the vent. Bring the lower part of the lining that is loose up toward the shoulders (Figure 52).
8. Line up all cut edges at the top edge of the vent (Figure 53). Stitch across the top of the vent, ending one stitch past the edge of the underlap; backstitch. Make sure you don't stitch though the garment fabric because the stitches would show on the right side of the garment.
9. Clip diagonally into the corner of the lining at the last stitches (Figure 54), then bring the neckline of the lining up to meet the garment neckline and position the lower, unstitched portion of the lining on the vent turnback (Figure 55).
10. With right sides together, stitch the lining edge to the edge of the vent turnback almost down to the mitered corner. You will attach the remainder of the hem later.

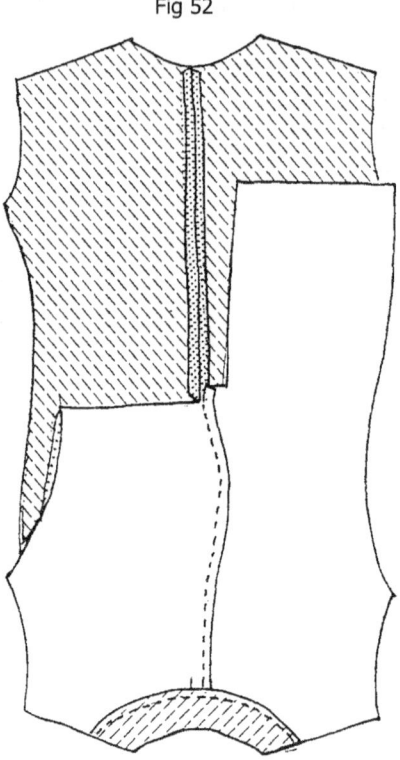

Fig 52

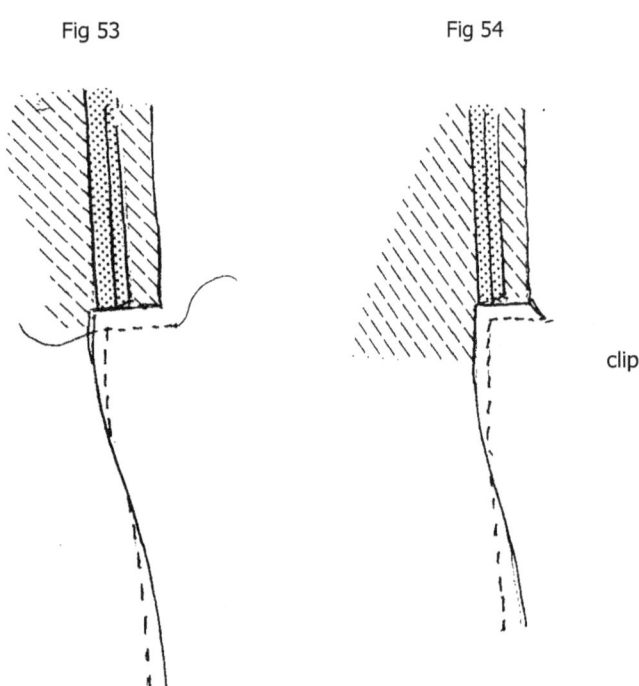

Fig 53   Fig 54

clip

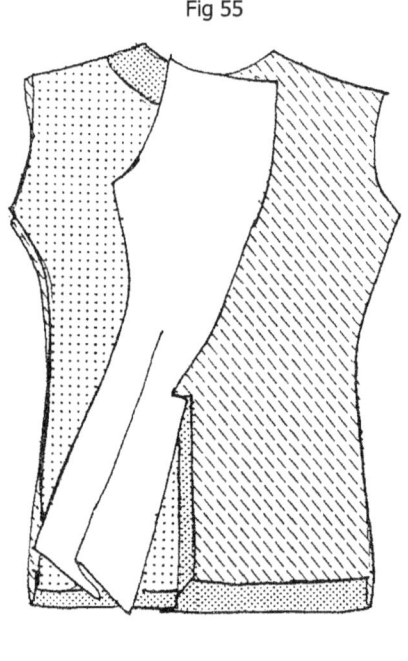

Fig 55

Attaching the Facings

Before you begin, check the neckline and front edges of the jacket fronts and facings to be sure that the opposite sides are identical and the edges are cleanly cut. Carefully trim away any raveled yarns so that you have a clean edge.

1. With right sides together, pin the facing to the jacket front at the break point where there are jogs in the seam allowances. Force the jog back until both cut edges are even, and place pins to hold the jog in line. Pin from the jog to the hem (Figure 56).
2. Returning to the jog at the break point, you will find a jog in the seam allowance of the facing. Again, force the jog so that the cut edges are even and pin in place. Pin the remainder of the lapel area, easing at the lapel point (On the facing) to the collar termination point (Figure 57).
3. Stitch the pinned seam using a ⅜"-wide (1 cm) seam allowance. *Do not clip into the seam at the collar notch unless absolutely necessary* (Figure 58). Note: The illustration shows 2" (5 cm) strips of fusible web on the wrong side of the facing in the bust area and close to the hem. Baste these in place *only after completing the next steps.*
4. Turn right side out and check the lapels and front edges. At the break point of the lapel, the seam should curve in an "S" and make the front edge roll toward the facing below the break point and toward the jacket above the break point. Turn wrong side out.
5. Press the seam open working over a point presser and/or pressing ham.
6. Trim the seam allowance of the *jacket front* to ³⁄₁₆" (5 mm) from the break point down and around the curve at the hem.
7. Trim the seam allowance of the *facing* to ³⁄₁₆" (5 mm) from the break point up and around the lapel point.

Note: This method of trimming differs from the directions commonly given in other tailoring books and pattern guide sheets.

8. Turn the jacket right side out and press the lapels and front edges, carefully rolling the edges to the underside (toward the facing below the break point and toward the jacket in the lapel).
9. Baste the fusible web strips to the wrong side of the facing as shown in Figure 58.

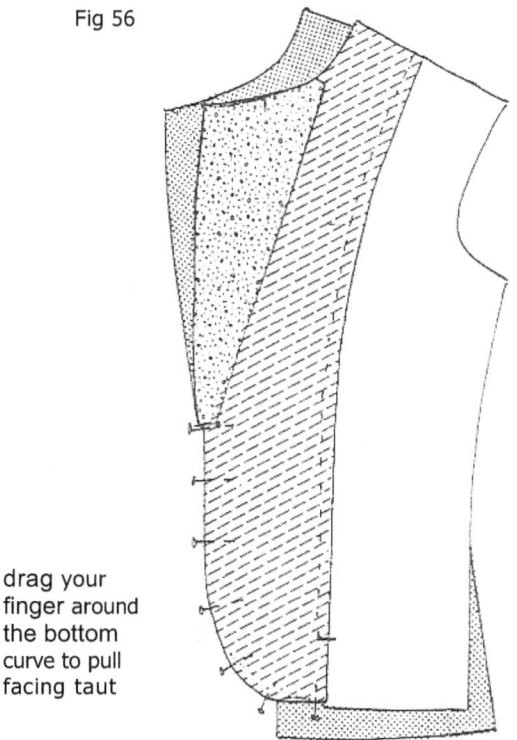

Fig 56

drag your finger around the bottom curve to pull facing taut

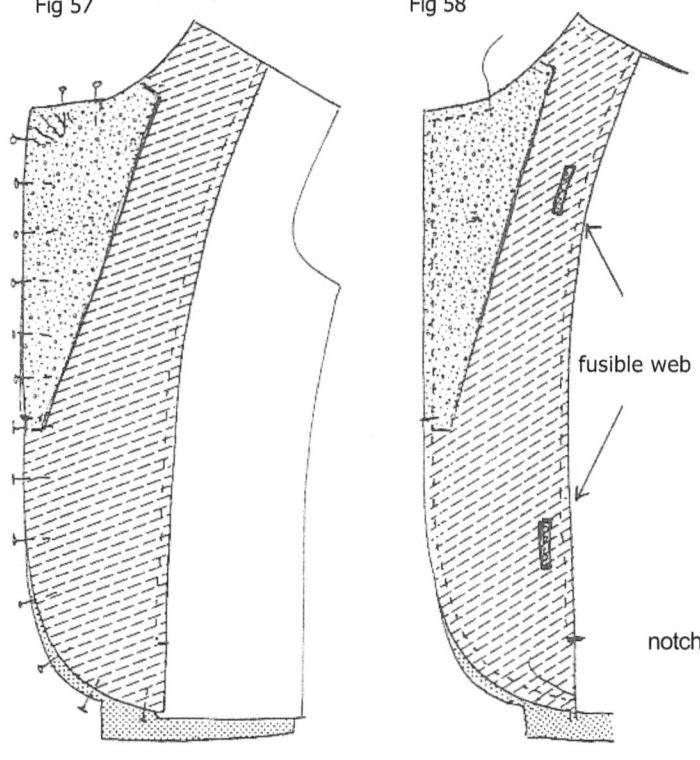

Fig 57

Fig 58

fusible web

notch

ADDING THE COLLAR

1. With right sides together, sew the jacket fronts to the jacket back at the shoulders. Press the seams open.
    Repeat with the lining.
2. Secure the collar to the collar termination points using the four-corner tie (one of the techniques used in traditional Japanese sewing to secure the kimono sleeve to the body of the garment).
    a. Thread a needle with thread to match the jacket fabric and double it.
    b. Place the collar inside the jacket neckline (with the jacket inside out).
    c. Insert the needle into the seam allowance of the jacket front neckline *exactly* at the termination point.
    d. Next, insert the needle into the undercollar seam allowance at the point where the collar attaches to the neckline.
    e. Insert the needle through the upper collar seam allowance opposite the same point on the undercollar.
    f. Bring the needle through to the collar termination point of the front facing.
    g. Without pulling the thread all the way to the knot, reverse the direction of the needle and go back in the opposite direction, inserting the needle through all the previous points.
    h. Carefully pull the thread to secure the corner of the collar to the neckline. Tie a square knot at the location where the needle first entered the jacket front (Figure 59).
3. Pin the upper collar to the facing neckline and the undercollar to the jacket neckline (Figure 60).
4. Stitch the collars to the neckline, starting at either the center back and working to the termination points, or starting at the termination points and stitching toward center back. Use a ⅜"-wide (1 cm) seam allowance.

Note: Stitching the collars to the necklines in a circular direction creates a drag away from one end of the collar toward the opposite end of the collar. This results in a lopsided look to the collar/lapel unit.

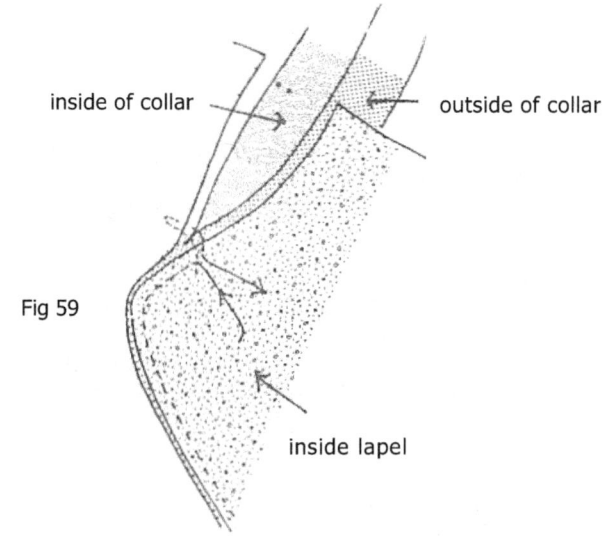

Fig 59

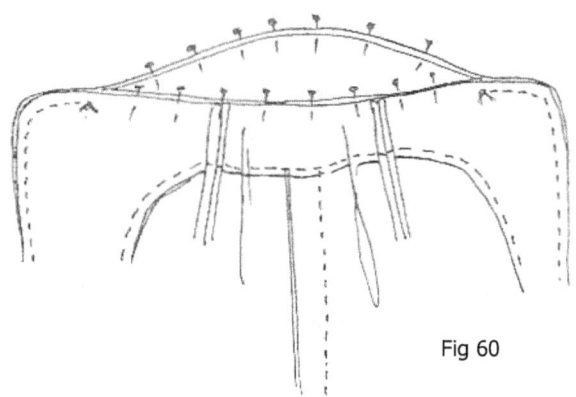

Fig 60

5. Press seams open, *clipping only as necessary* at the notch and around the neckline curve.
6. Baste the neckline seams of the jacket and the facing together by hand.
7. Topstitch or edgestitch around the fronts and collar to keep edges permanently in place. Begin and end stitching at the bottom of the facing. For examples of top stitching, see the illustrations on pages 26 and 68.

Note: You may leave this step until the end of the jacket construction if you prefer. Sometimes, the jacket designer will specify that edges have no stitching. In this case the manufacturer may fuse the layers together to keep them from separating.

8. Roll the collar and lapel into their finished position and give them a light pressing without pressing a sharp crease along the roll line.

FITTING THE LINING TO THE JACKET

1. Arrange the lining in the jacket.
2. Make sure the lining fits the jacket comfortably without pulling or bunching. If necessary, let out the darts and seams for a better fit.
3. Pin and stitch the side seams of the jacket. Press seams open.
4. Pin and stitch the side seams of the lining. Press the seams open or toward the jacket back.
5. Reach between the lining and the jacket at the armhole and pull the lining/jacket hem sections that have not yet been stitched through. Stitch the lining to the jacket hem, but leave the front corners unstitched. You will attach these later by hand.
6. Hand tack the hem to any available seams in the jacket to hold the hem in place.

INSERTING THE SLEEVES

1. Set your machine for a basting length stitch and stitch around the cap of the sleeve on the seamline. Start and end the stitching about 2" (5cm) from the underarm point. Repeat on the lining sleeve cap.
2. Pin shoulder pads inside the garment in the correct position. Put the garment on a dress form to hang the sleeves in the armholes.
3. Turning under the sleeve along the easestitching, pin the sleeve to the jacket armhole, drawing up ease as needed to fit the sleeve into the armhole. Check to make sure it hangs with the grainline perpendicular to the floor. Adjust as necessary, then chalk mark several balance points (for matching purposes) on the sleeve and jacket armhole before removing the sleeves (Figure 61).
4. Place the sleeve cap on a pressing ham and shrink out the ease, using steam and the point of the iron. Press out any tucks or ripples in the seam allowance that were caused by the ease stitches (Figure 62).

Note: If using fairly thin shoulder pads (¼" or thinner), proceed to step 5. If using thicker pads, proceed to the alternate method below.

5. Make sure the shoulder pads are correctly positioned in the shoulder of the jacket. Without removing the pads, pin the lining in place around the armhole so that the edges of the seam of the lining, shoulder pad and the garment are all even. This gives the lining, which was cut larger than the jacket, the necessary ease for comfort and wearability.
6. Permanently baste the lining to the armhole by hand, stitching through all layers including the shoulder pads.
7. Matching the balance marks you made earlier, pin each sleeve into the jacket armhole. Baste, then stitch slowly and carefully through the layers.
8. Trim the underarm section of the armhole to ¼" (6 mm) from notch to notch (Figure 63).
9. Optional: Insert a sleeve cap header (a 2" x 8" bias strip of self fabric or lambswool). This cushions the seam and/or gives some roundness to the sleeve cap. To insert the header, fold lengthwise so one half of it is wider than the other and catch to the stitching line with the wider half against the sleeve cap (Figure 64).

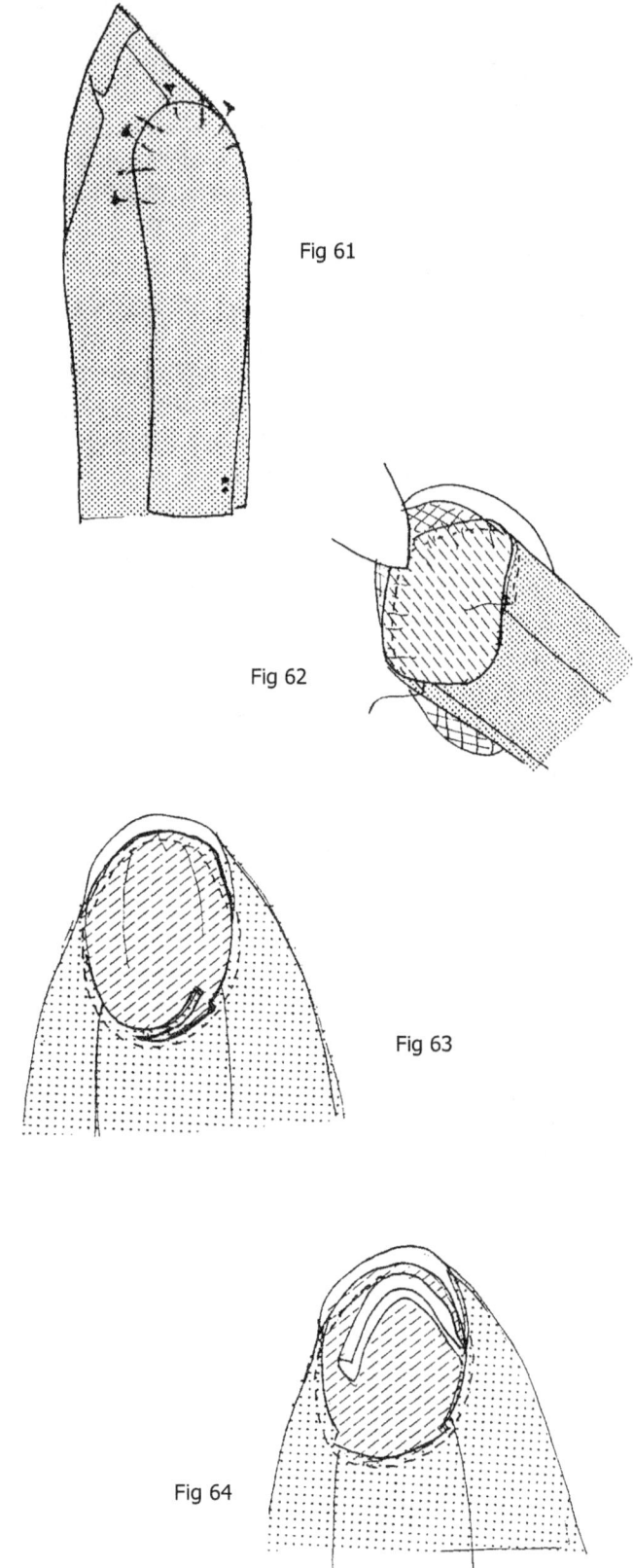

Fig 61

Fig 62

Fig 63

Fig 64

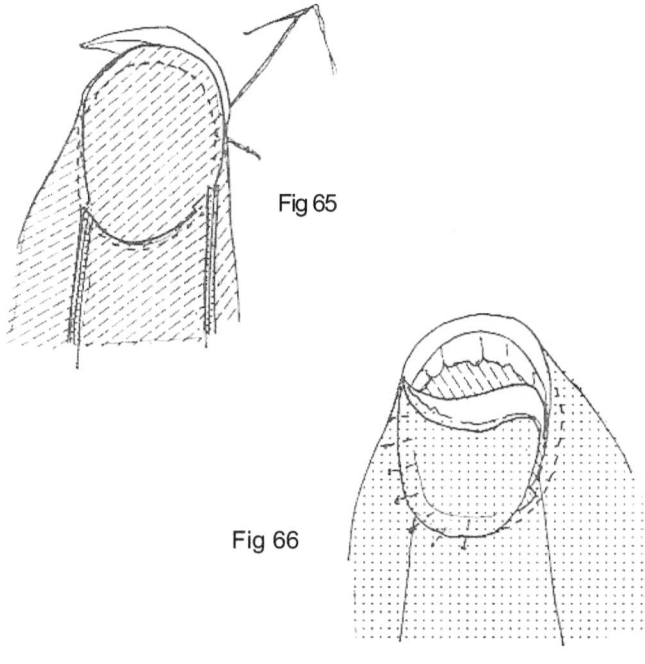

Fig 65

Fig 66

Alternative Method for Sleeve Insertion

1. Remove the shoulder pads and pin the sleeves into the garment armholes, carefully matching the balance marks made earlier. Baste and stitch permanently.
2. Press the seam allowance of the sleeve/armhole, making sure all wrinkles and ease are satisfactorily remove.
3. Sew the shoulder pads to the shoulder seams and to the armhole seams, using a double strand of waxed thread and a ½"-long (1.3 cm) running stitch. Keep the edge of the pad even with the cut edges of the sleeve and armhole (Figure 65).
4. Optional: Insert a sleeve cap header as shown in step 10, above.
5. Pin the armhole of the jacket lining to the armhole so that all cut edges are even. Permanently baste the lining to the armhole.
6. Trim the underarm seam to ¼" (6 mm) from notch to notch as shown in Figure 63, above.

Finishing the Jacket

1. Turn under the sleeve cap seam allowance in each lining sleeve and pin to the armhole, distributing ease around the armhole. The turned edge of the sleeve should just cover the permanent basting stitches that hold the jacket lining to the armhole (Figure 66).
2. Hand stitch the sleeve lining to the armhole with a felling stitch. As you stitch, catch the seam allowance of the jacket and the lining, rather than catching only the lining. This securely anchors the sleeve lining to the jacket armhole (Figure 67).
3. Stitch the front edges of the lining hem by hand (Figure 68).
4. Make buttonholes by hand or machine.
5. Sew buttons in position.
6. Give the garment a final press, carefully maintaining the roll of the collar and lapel. *Do not crease the lapel but let it roll naturally.* Now is the time to press the strips of fusible webbing shown in Figure 58 on page 29 in place.

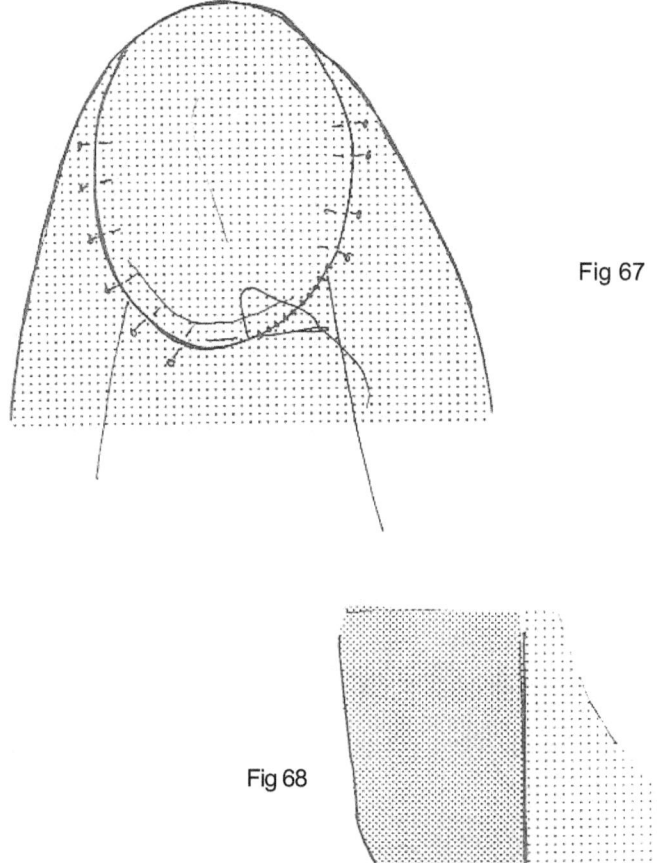

Fig 67

Fig 68

JACKET POCKETS

Pockets are one of the most visible signs of the overall quality of a tailored garment. Therefore, they must be precisely constructed, paying close attention to detail. The location of the pocket is an important factor to consider before applying them. Placement depends on whether the pockets are decorative or functional. Decorative pockets should be positioned where they are most pleasing to the eye. Be aware of proportion and how the pocket placement contributes to the overall look of the garment. Functional pockets should be placed at a level that is comfortable for the hand to reach.

The top edge of *horizontal pockets* should be placed two-thirds of one's sleeve length, measuring down from the armpits, or about 2" lower than half the distance between the bustline and the hem edge (Figures 69 and 70).

Vertical pockets usually start 1 ½" to 2" (4 to 5 cm) below the waistline and are about 5" to 7" (12.7 to 18 cm) long. The inner top corner is located about 1" (2.5 cm) to the side of the classic princess seamline (Figure 71).

The top edge of a *patch pocket* should be placed about 2 ½" to 3" (6.5 to 7.5 cm) below the waistline and set back 3" to 4 ½" (7.5 to 11.5 cm) from the center front, depending on their size and shape (Figure 72).

Breast pockets are usually about 3 ½" (9 cm) long and are located with forward point on the bustline. They should slant up about ¾" (2 cm) at the end that is closer to the armhole (Figure 69).

When determining the position for lower pockets, keep these points in mind:

1. As the coat or jacket gets longer, the pocket placement should get proportionately lower.
2. The pocket style dictates the level of the cut (the opening that is cut into the garment for the pocket). Welts sit on top of the cut line and flaps sit below the cut line. This means that the cut for welt must be lower than the cut for the flap (Figure 73).
3. For level-cut horizontal pockets, the front corner should be ⅛" (3 mm) higher than the side corner. For the slant cut, pivot at the center of the pocket level and angle it to suit your taste. The usual slant is ¾" (2 cm) and the opening should become longer as the slant gets longer (Figure 74).

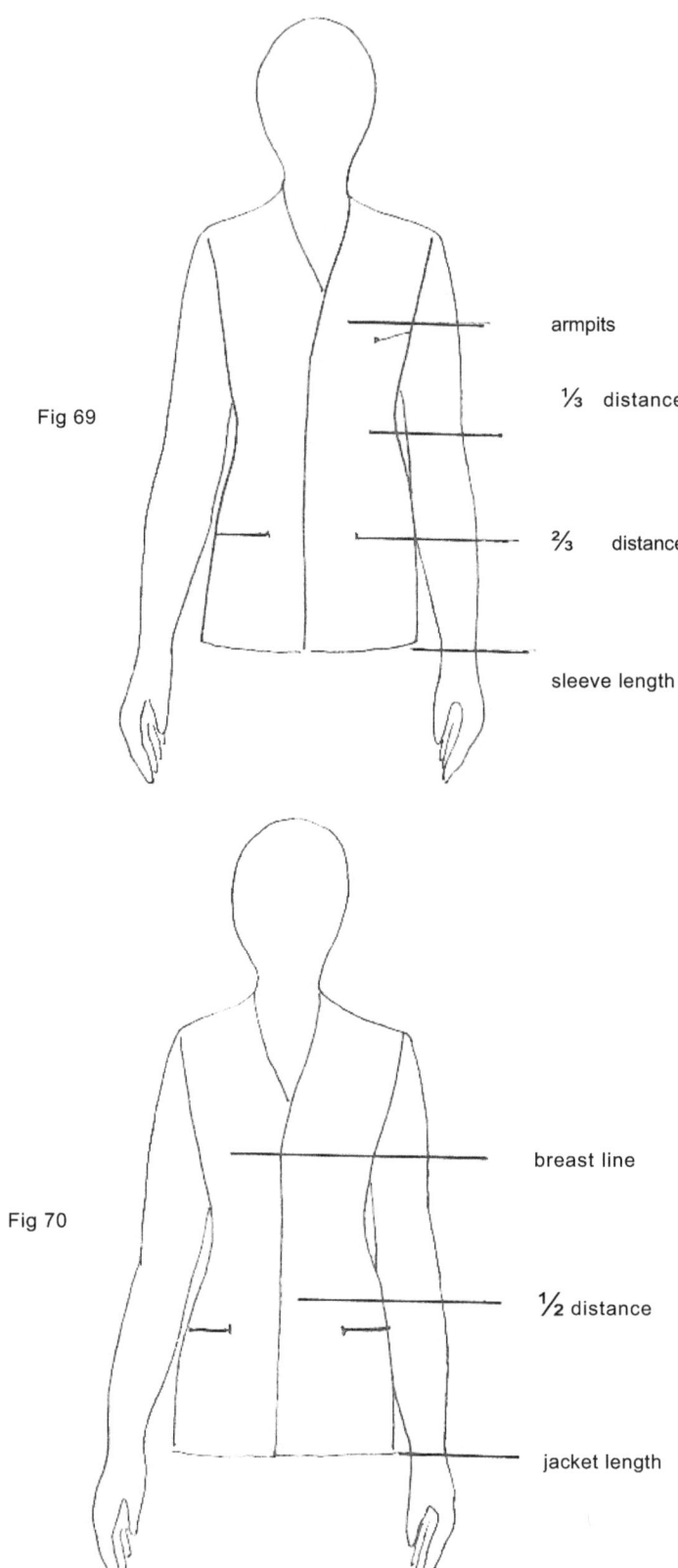

Fig 69

Fig 70

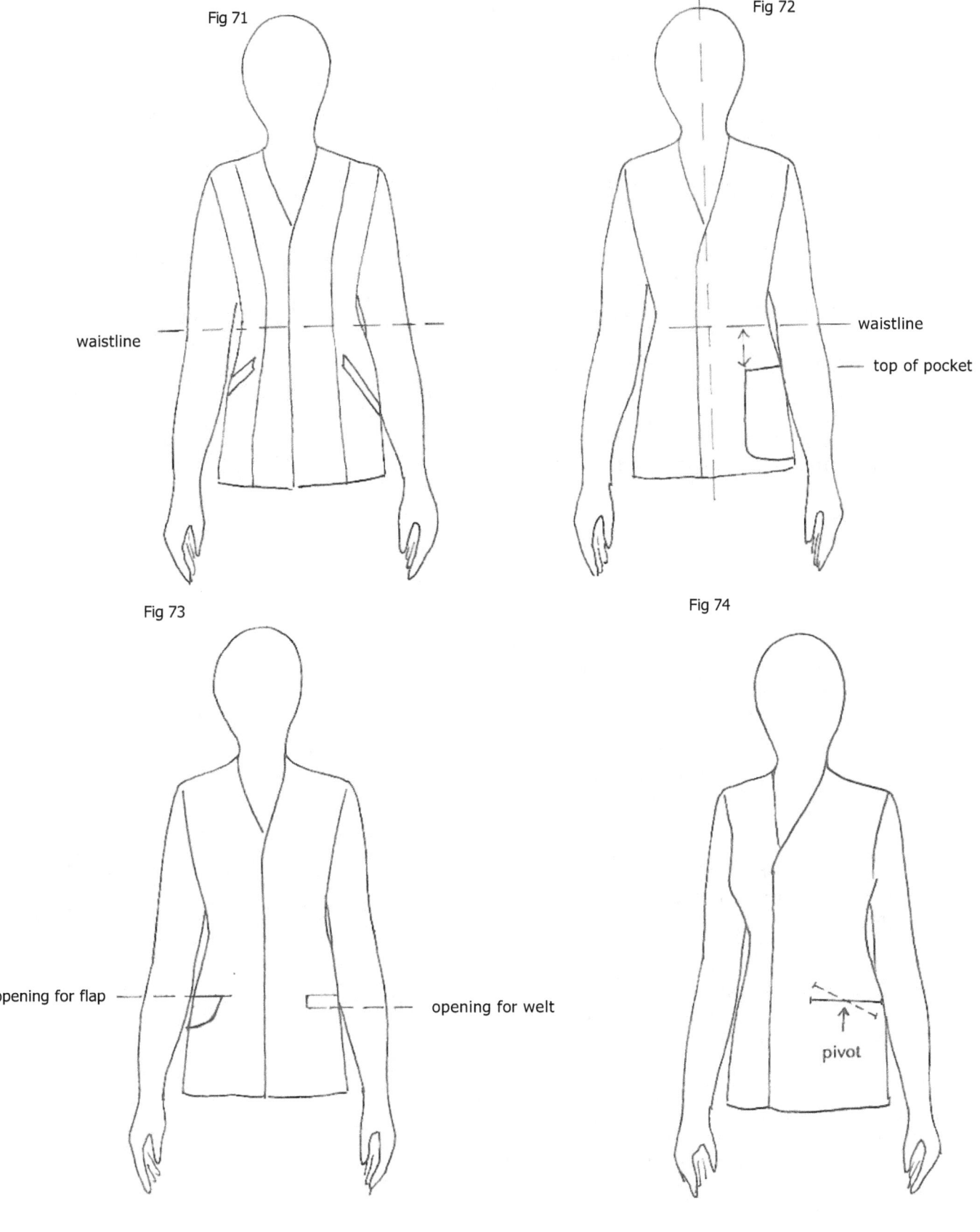

Double Welt Pockets

Welt pockets are a hallmark of finely tailored coats and jackets. They are not difficult as long as you take the time to mark the pocket locations precisely and stitch accurately. To make sure that both pockets are the same, mark the pocket location with tailor tacks before removing the pattern tissue and separating the fabric layers.

Welt pocket openings are, on the average, about 5" to 5 ½" (12.5 to 14 cm) for women and from 6" to 6 ½" (15 to 16.5 cm) for men.

Cutting

Cut one of each of the following pieces for each pocket:

Upper pocket bag: 5" x 7" (12.5 cm x 18 cm) piece of pocketing for women, or 6" x 8" (15cm x 20cm) for men

Under pocket bag: 7" x 7" (15 cm x 18 cm) piece of fashion fabric for women, or 8" x 8" (20 cm x 20 cm) for men

Pocket welt: 4" x 7" (10 cm x 18 cm) piece of fashion fabric for women, or 4" x 8" (10 cm x 20 cm) for men

Pocket facing: 2 ½" x 7" (6.5 cm x 18 cm) piece of fashion fabric for women and 2 ½" x 8" for men

Reinforcing stay: 2" x 7" (5 cm x 18 cm) piece of muslin or fusible interfacing for women, or 2" x 8" (5 cm x 20 cm) for men

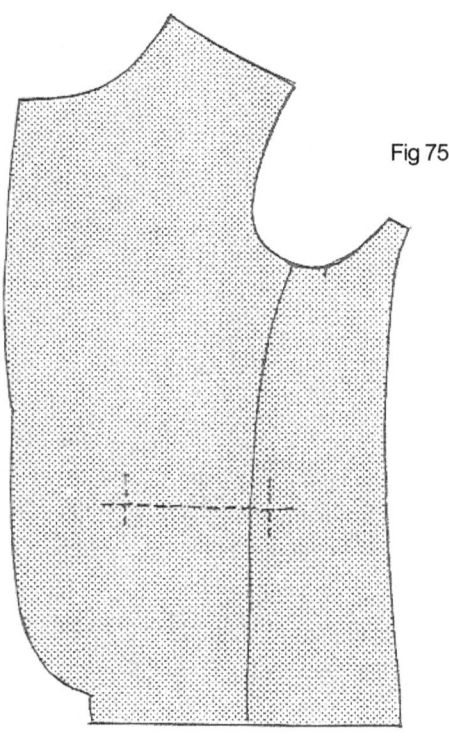

Fig 75

Construction

1. Place the stay over the pocket marking on the wrong side of the garment and baste or fuse into place.
2. Mark the center of the pocket opening and the ends with short basting stitches on the garment fronts, stitching through the jacket and the stay (Figure 75).
3. Using a sharp pencil or chalk, draw the exact shape and size of the pocket opening on each side of the center line on the stay (Figure 76).
4. With chalk, draw a line on the wrong side of the welt 1 ½" (4 cm) from and parallel to the upper long edge.
5. Place the welt face down on the right side of the garment with the center line of the pocket matching the line on the welt. Pin in place. The wider portion of the welt should be below the pocket line.

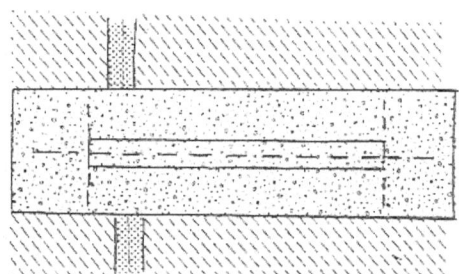

Fig 76

6. Turn the garment to the wrong side and using the lines on the stay as a guide, machine stitch on the two long lines only. Do not stitch past the ends of the lines. Backstitch carefully or leave a length of thread for tying (Figure 77).
7. Slash the welt only, cutting down the exact center from end to end so that it is in two pieces (Figure 78).
8. To cut the pocket opening in the garment, slash the stay and garment between the two rows of stitching. Cut at an angle into the corners at each end (Figure 77).
9. Press open the seams that were formed by the cut, placing an edge board under the seam (Figure 79).
10. Fold the welt pieces over each of the opening seams and hand haste in the ditch to hold them in place (Figure 80).
11. Baste the edges of the welts together with diagonal basting stitches (Figure 81).
12. With the garment right side up, fold it back along the seam holding the lower welt to the garment and machine stitch along the original stitching. This holds the welt permanently in place. With right sides together, stitch the pocket bag cut from pocketing fabric to the lower edge of the welt, using a ¼"-wide (6 mm) seam allowance. Press the seam toward the pocket bag (Figure 82).

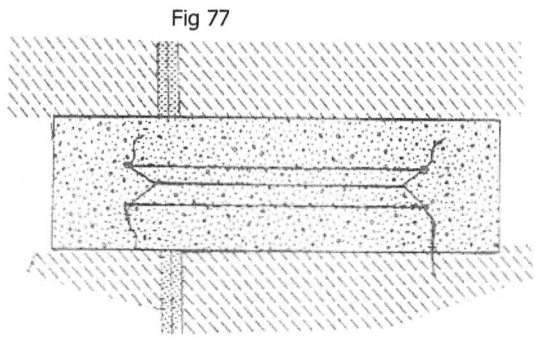
Fig 77

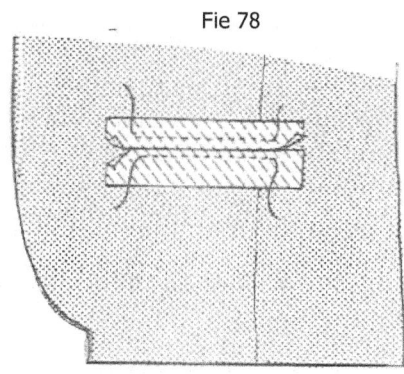
Fie 78

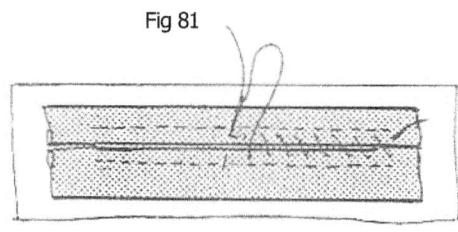
Fig 81

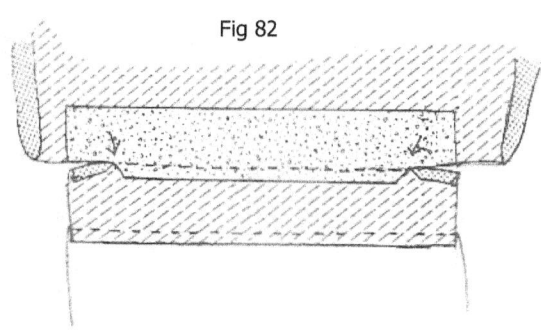
Fig 82

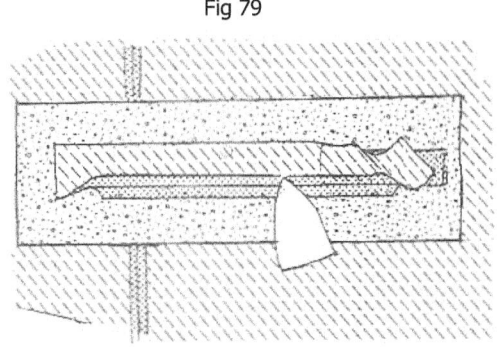
Fig 79

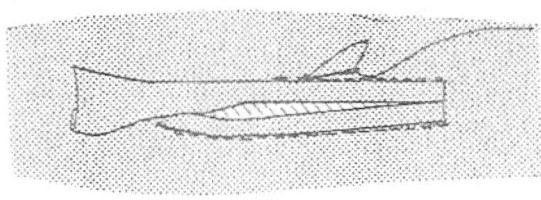
Fig 80

13. Fold the triangles under at each end and anchor in place (Figure 83).
14. With right sides together, pin the fashion fabric under pocket to the upper pocket (Figure 84).
15. Turn the garment over, then fold it out of the way so you can stitch across the triangle at the end of the welt again. Turn the corner and stitch across the top on the original stitching to permanently stitch the upper welt in place (Figure 85). At the end of the welt, turn the corner again, stitch across the remaining triangle. Before completing the pocket stitching, pin out a tiny tuck in the upper pocket (pocketing fabric). This helps prevent the finished pocket from gaping open..
16. Continue stitching down and around the bottom of the pocket (Figure 86),and up to the starting point.
17. Trim and grade the pocket seams to eliminate bulk where necessary.
18. Leave the basting in the welts until the garment is completed.

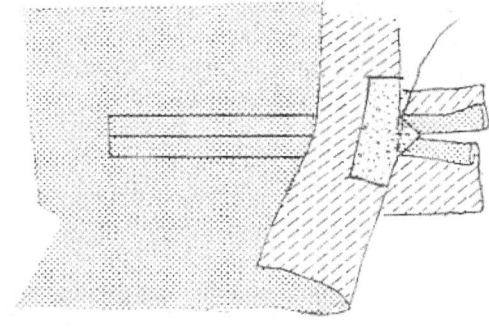

Fig 83

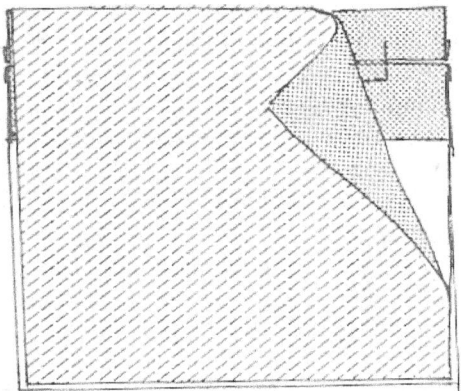

Fig 84

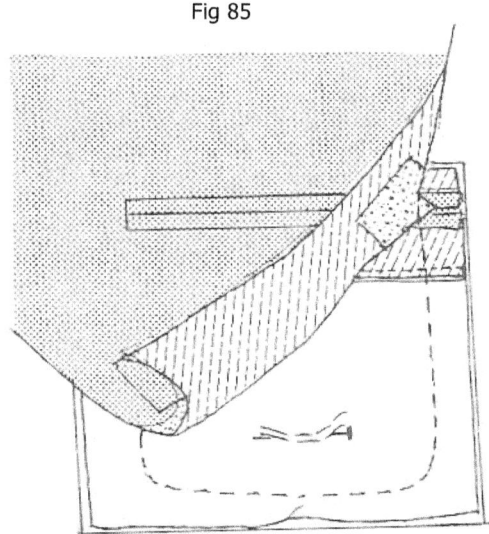

Fig 85

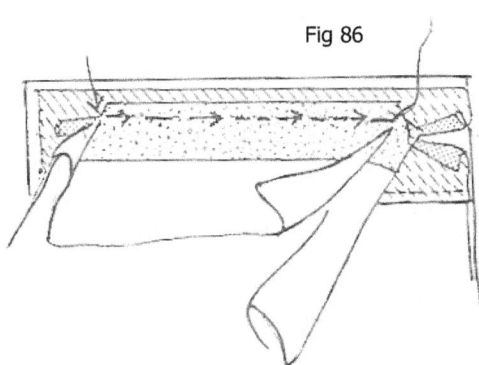

Fig 86

Flap Pocket

The flap of the pocket covers a lower welt. Like the double welt pocket, it requires careful marking, stitching, and cutting.

Cutting

Cut one of each of following pieces per pocket:

Upper pocket bag: 5" x 7" (12.5 cm x 18 cm) piece of pocketing fabric, or 6" x 8" (15 cm x 20 cm) for men.

Under pocket bag: 7" x 7" (15 cm x 18 cm) piece of either pocketing fabric or fashion fabric for women; for men, cut an 8" x 8" (20 cm x 20 cm) piece of pocketing fabric.

Welt: 3" x 7" (7.5 cm x 18 cm) piece of fashion fabric for women, or 3" x 8" (7.5 cm x 20 cm) for men

Reinforcing stay: 2" x 8" (5cm x 20cm) piece of muslin or fusible interfacing

Flap: Cut 1 of the desired size and shape from fashion fabric and one from lining fabric (for the flap facing). Cut with ¼" - wide (6 mm) seam allowances on all edges. You may use an existing flap pattern piece, if available. Trim the seam allowances on the pattern tissue to ¼" before cutting from the fabrics.

Facing: 3" x 7" for women, 3" x 8" for men

Construction

1. Trim $1/16$" (1 mm) from the outer edges of the flap facing (lining fabric) but *do not trim the top edge of the facing.* Pin facing to the flap with raw edges even. Because you trimmed the facing the flap will be slightly larger. Stitch ¼" (6 mm) from the outer raw edges. Clip across square corners and notch round corners to eliminate bulk (Figure 87). Press the seam open on the edge board before turning right side out. The facing should barely roll to the underside of the flap so it doesn't show from the right side. Press. Edge stitch by hand or machine.
2. Draw a chalk line on the lining side of the flap, parallel to the bottom edge of the flap and ¼" from the upper raw edges (Figure 88).
3. With right sides together, stitch the welt to the upper pocket bag, using a ¼" - wide (6mm) seam allowance. Press the seam toward the pocket bag (Figure 89).
4. Cut a 3" -wide strip of lining fabric the width of the under pocket bag for the facing. Turn under ¼" along the bottom edge. Place the lining on top of the under pocket bag with the upper raw edges even. Edgestitch in place at the turned edge (Figure 90).

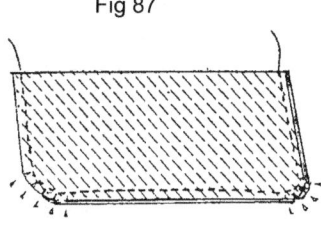

Fig 87

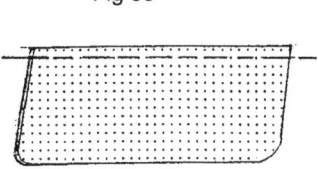

Fig 88

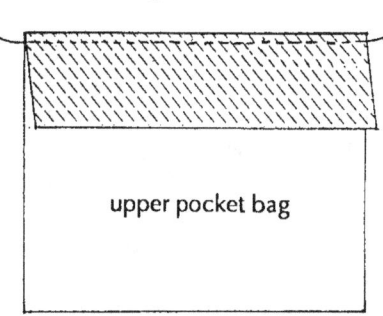

Fig 89

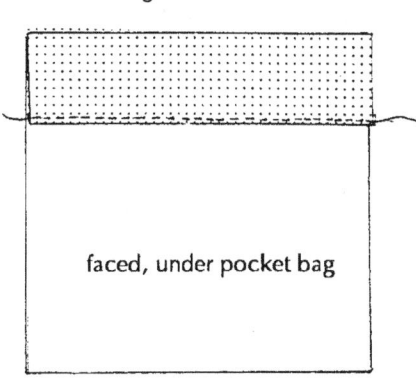

Fig 90

5. On the wrong side of the garment, center the stay over the pocket location marks. Fuse or baste in place.
6. Hand baste along the exact pocket opening. The upper line should be the same length as the line you drew on the pocket flap facing. The lower line should be parallel to the upper line and exactly ½" (1.2 cm) away. It should be ⅛" (3 mm) shorter than the upper line at each end (Figure 91). For example, if the upper line is 5" (12.5 cm) long, the lower line should be 4 ¾" long (12 cm).

Fig 91

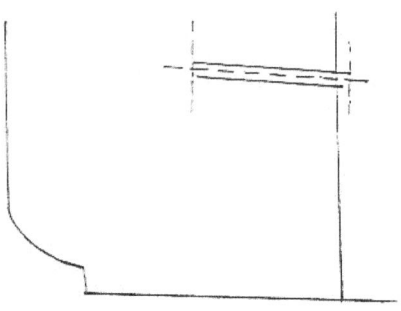

7. Draw a chalk line on the wrong side of the welt, ¼" (6 mm) from the top long edge and the same length as the lower pocket opening line on the garment.
8. Draw a chalk line on the reverse side of the under pocket piece ¼" (6 mm) from the upper raw edge and the same length as the line on the flap.
9. Place the welt/upper pocket bag face down on the right side of the garment with the chalk line exactly on top of the lower opening line. Pin or baste in place.

Place the flap (dashed lines in the illustration) on the garment face down with the chalk line on the flap exactly on top of the upper opening line. Pin or baste in place.

Place the facing side of the under pocket on top of the flap with lines matching. Pin or baste in place (Figure 92).

Fig 92

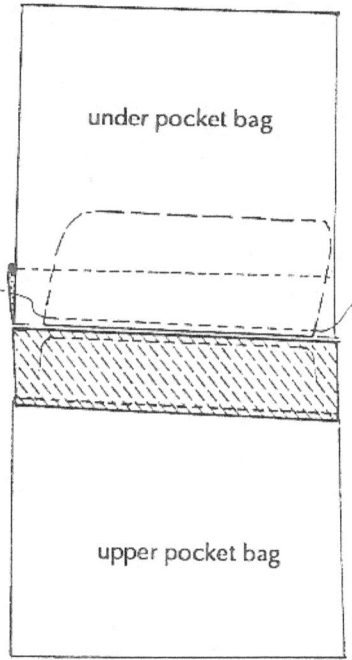

10. Machine stitch on the chalked lines, stitching on the top line first and then on the welt. Begin and end stitching with careful backstitching, or leave thread tails for tying.
11. On the wrong side, cut through the stay and garment between the two rows of stitching and cut at an angle into the corners at each end (Figure 93).
12. Press the lower seam open and leave the upper seam as stitched (Figure 94).

*Edge stitch or top stitch flap before setting into pocket, if desired.**

Fig 94

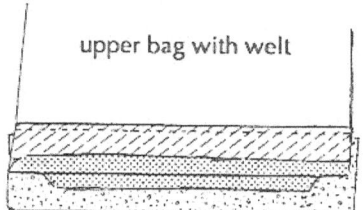

Fig 93

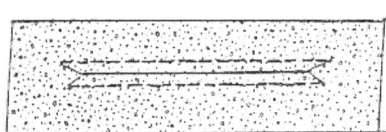

13. Fold the welt over the seam allowance so that the welt exactly fills the ½" (1.2 cm) opening between the two rows of stitching. Baste in the ditch to hold the welt in place (Figure 95).
14. With the garment right side up, fold the garment back along the basted welt seam. Machine stitch through the stay and the welt close to the first line of stitching (Figure 96).
15. Place the welt under the flap and pin the opening closed. The seam allowance of the flap and the pocketing should point up.
16. Fold the garment back to expose the triangles at each end of the pocket and machine stitch in place. With the garment right side up, fold it out of the way to expose the triangles and the pocket bags. Pin out a tiny tuck in the upper pocket (pocketing fabric). This helps prevent the finished pocket from gaping open. Stitch across the triangle and continue stitching down and around the pocket bag and across the triangle at the opposite end of the pocket (Figure 97).
17. Turn the flap up out of the way and edgestitch the short seam at each end of the pocket. Then bartack with silk buttonhole twist to cover the stitching. This helps to stabilize the ends of the pocket opening (Figure 98).
18. On the inside, grade the seam allowances to eliminate unnecessary bulk.

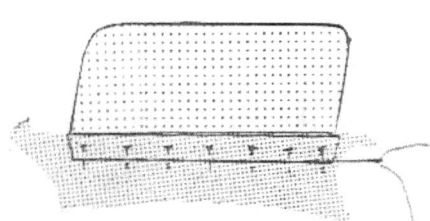

Fig 95

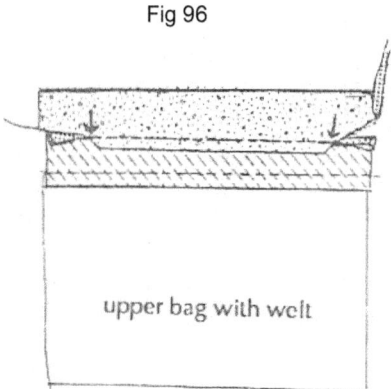

Fig 96

upper bag with welt

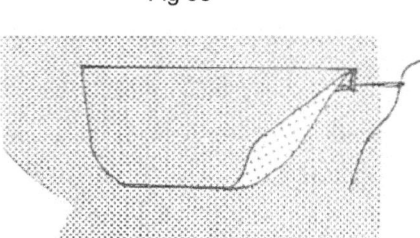

Fig 98

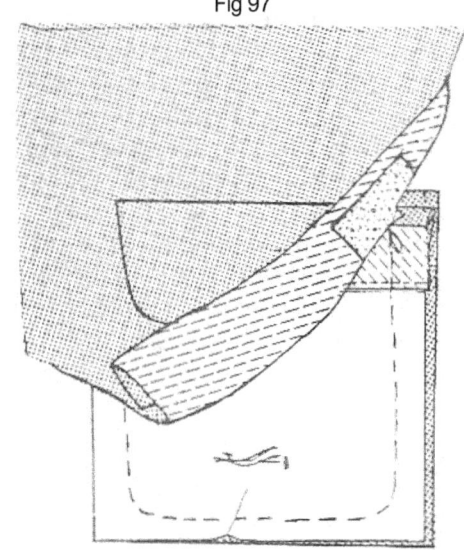

Fig 97

INSIDE – STITCHED PATCH POCKET

This method of applying patch pockets is most often used by menswear manufacturers and tailors. The patches are stitched to the coat or jacket fronts from inside the patches so that the stitching is completely hidden from view. The lack of topstitching gives this patch pocket a very dressy appearance. If you want edgestitched or topstitched patch pockets instead, follow the construction method on page 30, which is much easier than this method for patch pockets.

CUTTING AND CONSTRUCTION

1. For each pocket, cut a pocket from the fashion fabric and a pocket lining from the lining fabric. Use a pocket pattern of your choice and trim all seams to a width of ¼".

2. Cut a piece of edge tape the length of the top edge of the pocket. Machine stitch the tape to the wrong side of the pocket, just above the hem fold line (Figure 99).

3. With right sides together, machine stitch the lining to the pocket, using a ¼"-wide (6 mm) seam allowance. Press the seam toward the lining. Turn the pocket lining to the inside along the pocket hem line and pin the layers together with wrong sides facing. Machine baste through both layers ⅛ (3 mm) outside the seam line. Trim, leaving a ¼"-wide (6 mm) seam allowance around the pocket (Figure 100).

4. Place the patch pocket right side up on the garment in the desired position. Chalk mark the outline of the patch onto the garment front. Be sure to test the chalk to make sure you can remove it from the fabric and permanent marks will not remain. Chalk balance lines across the pocket edge and onto the garment for matching purposes (Figure 101).

   Remove the pocket and transfer the balance lines to the wrong side of the pocket. Extend the marks on the garment inward toward the center of the pocket location (Figure 102).

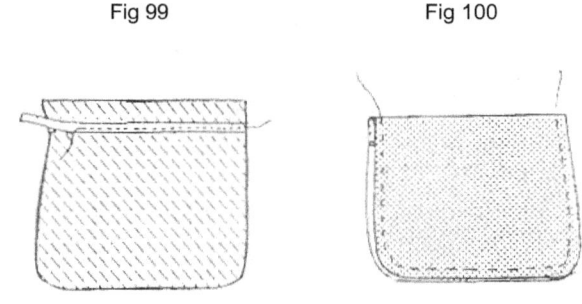

Fig 99   Fig 100

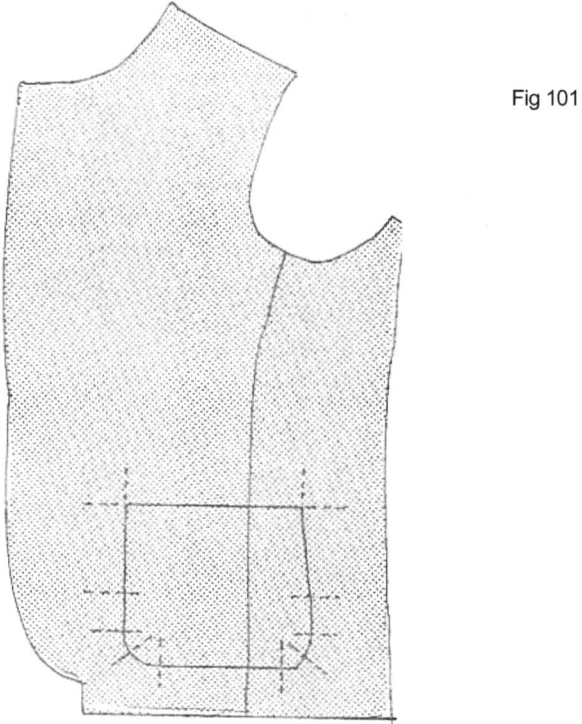

Fig 101

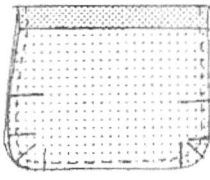

Fig 102

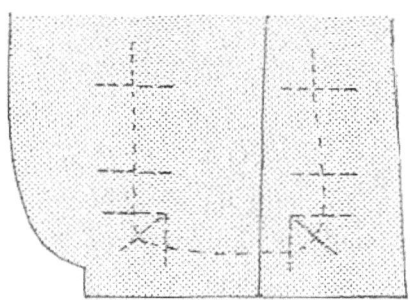

5. Chalk mark or baste-mark another outline of the pocket shape ⅝" (1.5 cm) away from and to the inside of the chalked pocket outline (Figure 103).
6. To reinforce the pocket corners, cut 1" squares of fusible interfacing and fuse to the wrong side of the garment, centering them over the upper corners of the pocket location.
7. To bag the pocket onto the garment, place it face down on the garment with the raw edge of the pocket against the inside outline and the balance lines matching. Begin stitching at the top edge of the pocket, using a ³⁄₁₆" (5 mm) seam allowance and continuing around to the other top edge. Match balance lines carefully as you stitch.

   Be sure to keep the raw edges of the patch lined up with the inside outline and maintain a uniform seam allowance width all the way around. Work slowly and carefully to ensure success (Figure 104).
8. Fold the seam allowances under at an angle at each side of the opening (Figure 105) and tack by hand from the inside using a double row of pad stitches (Figure 106).
9. Press the edges of the pocket so that they are flush against the machine stitching and do not fold over onto the garment piece.

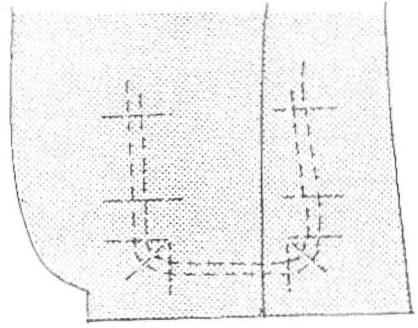

Fig 103

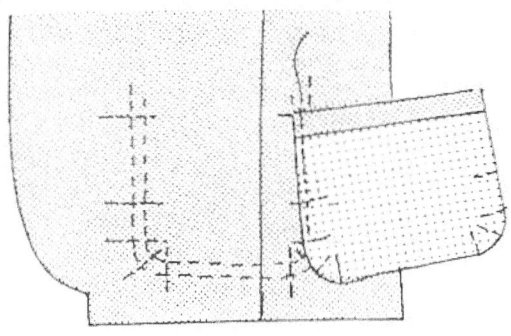

Fig 104

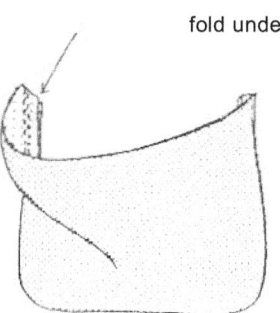

fold under

Fig 105

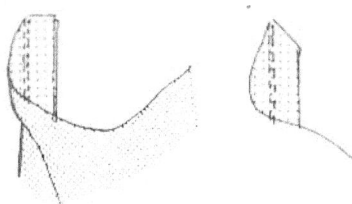

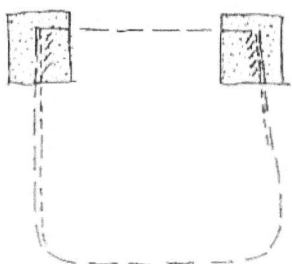

Fig 106

Alternate Patch Pocket Method

1. Complete steps 1-6 above.
2. Turn under and press the seam allowance around the pocket.
3. Position the pocket on the garment front and slip baste in place or use a very narrow zigzag stitch to baste the pocket in place (Figure 107).
4. Machine stitch in place inside the pocket. Press (Figure 108).

Inside Jacket Pocket

If only one inside pocket is desired, it is usually placed on the right side to balance the outside breast pocket, which is always on the left side. The level of the pocket is about 1 ¼" (3 cm) below the armscye, slanting down ¾" (2 cm) toward the center front. The opening may vary in length from 4 ½" to 6" (11.5 cm to 15 cm), depending on the size of the person.

Cutting

1. After the front facing has been attached to the front lining, chalk mark the desired length of the pocket opening onto the lining, extending it ½" (1.5 cm) into the front facing and slanting it as described above. See Figure 109.
2. Cut 1 piece of pocketing fabric 8" (20cm) wide and twice the desired length of the finished pocket, plus 2 ¾" (7 cm). Cut the top and bottom edges on the same slant as the pocket as shown in Figure 109. Cut 2 facing pieces from lining fabric, each 3" x 8" (7.5 x 20 cm), cutting them on the straight grain of the fabric.

Construction

1. Chalk mark a line the same length as the pocket opening line onto the wrong side of one of the facing pieces. Draw it 1¼" (3 cm) below the top edge. Chalk mark a line of the same length onto the wrong side of the pocketing 1¼" (3 cm) below the top edge. See Figure 109, above.
2. Place the pocketing face down on the table, then place the lining/facing on top with the right side facing up and chalked lines matching. Next, place the facing piece on top, right side down, again matching the chalked lines. Pin, then baste the layers together along the chalked line.
3. Machine stitch around the pocket, stitching 3/16" (5mm) away from and parallel to the chalked lines. Stitch across the ends (Figure 110).

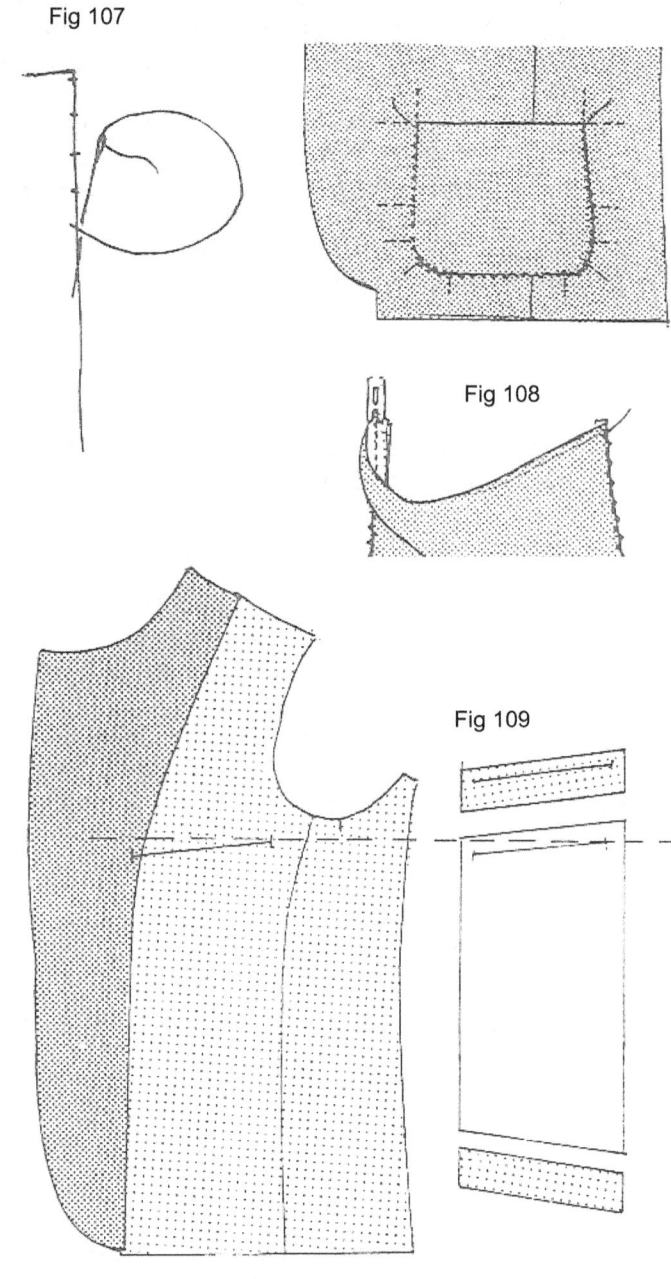

Fig 107

Fig 108

Fig 109

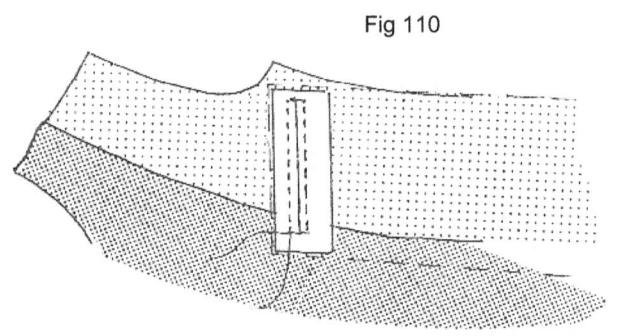

Fig 110

4. Slash through all layers halfway between the upper and lower stitching lines and at an angle into the corners at each end. Turn the facing piece to the inside, enveloping each cut edge to form the welts for the pocket opening. Pin or baste in place. Machine stitch the lower welt in place (Figure 111).

5. On the inside, turn under the long raw edges of the facing piece and stitch to the pocketing. Turn under and press ¼" (6 mm) along one long edge of the remaining pocket facing. Place it on top of the lower end of the pocketing with raw edges even. Machine stitch to the pocketing along the pressed edge (Figure 112).

6. Fold the bottom end of the pocketing up to form the pocket bag (Figure 113) and machine stitch from one end of the pocket, down around the bottom and back up to the remaining end of the pocket (Figure 114).

7. Permanently topstitch the pocket ends and the upper welt to the pocketing from the right side. Press. Trim seam allowances (Figure 115).

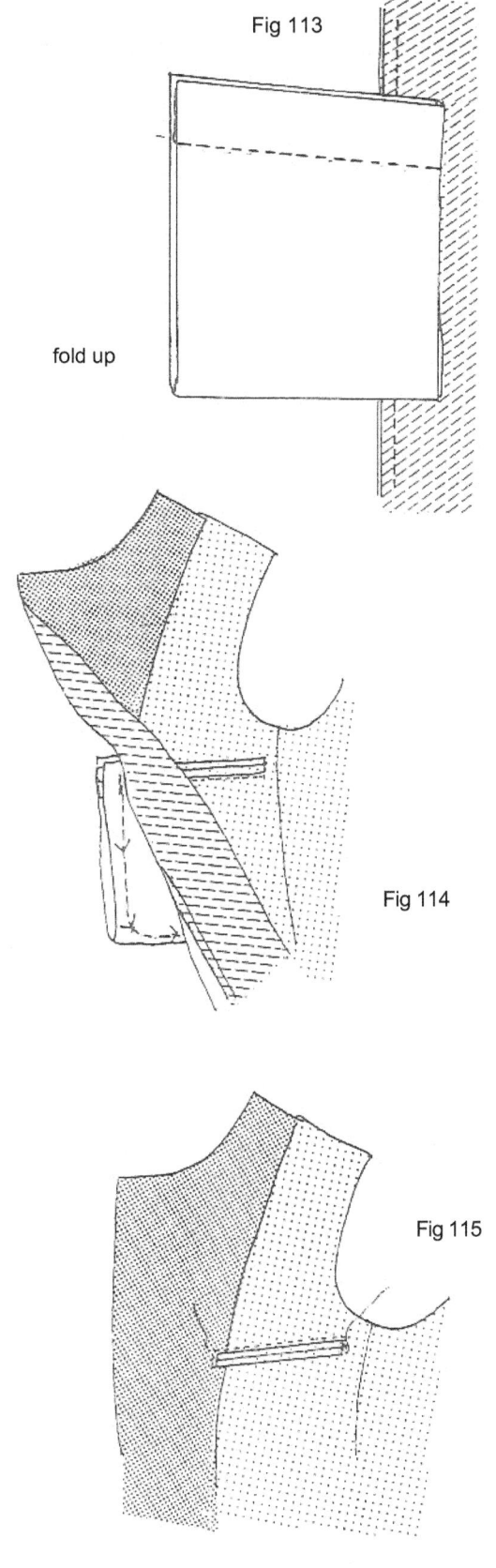

Fig 113

fold up

Fig 114

Fig 115

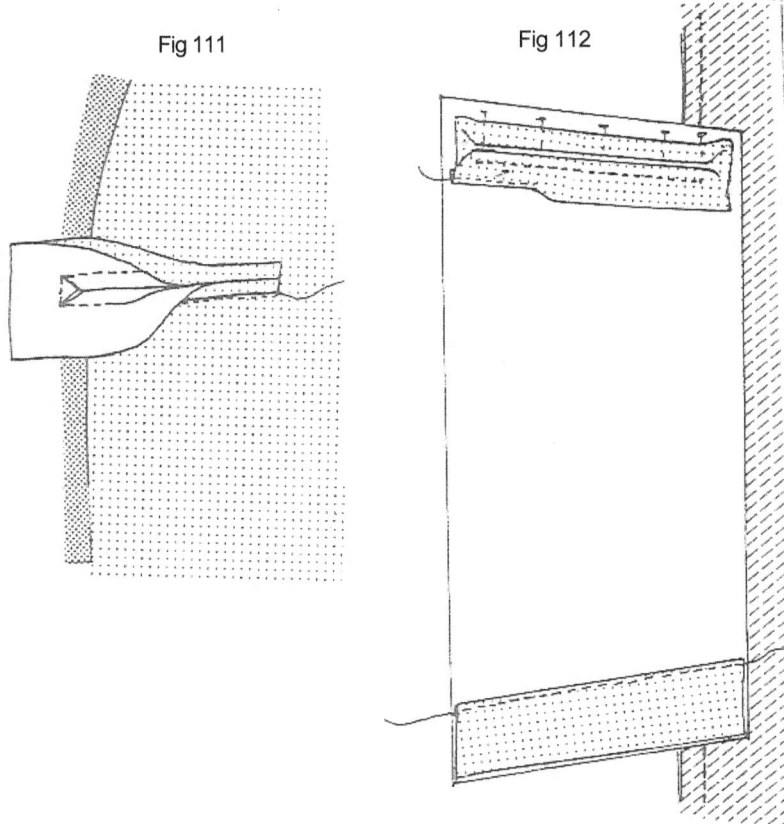

Fig 111

Fig 112

Notes

The Tailored Coat

The Tailored Coat, Simplified

Although more traditional tailoring has given way to the contemporary, ready-to-wear methods in the garment industry and in home sewing, many sewers continue to use the traditional methods that are the basis for all fine sewing. In this section, the emphasis is on combining tried and true traditional techniques with "quick tailoring" methods to economize on time and labor without sacrificing quality.

Fabric Selection

Fashion Fabric

Selecting fabric for a coat depends in part on design, style and the intended use. Since a coat is most often worn for warmth and protection, it usually requires a fabric that is heavier than that used for other garments. Coating fabrics include fleece, heavy tweeds, gabardine and other fabrics with twill weaves, heavy flannel and melton cloth. The choice of weight and weave density depends on style and design choices. An oversized, full style requires a lighter and/or more loosely woven fabric. Otherwise the finished coat will be too heavy and bulky to be comfortable. A more closely fitted coat looks skimpy and without substance unless you choose a heavier fabric.

Wool is the most popular fiber for coats because of its high absorbency and ability to provide warmth without too much weight.

Lining Fabric

A coat lining should be slick and slippery to slide easily over other clothing. It should have enough body and strength to be compatible with the heavier, outer fabric and to adequately protect and hide the inner construction. Synthetic fibers are most often used for lining fabrics because of their smoothness and strength. Among them, high-quality rayon and acetate are favored for their ability to "breathe". This makes them more comfortable to wear than polyester or nylon.

A twill weave is the most durable and is often chosen for a coat lining, rather than satin or plain-weave fabrics. Satin and taffeta work well in garments that stand out from the body, but they are too stiff and crisp to use for lining a more fitted garment. You may choose a backed lining fabric to provide extra warmth in a winter coat, but these fabrics are usually stiffer and bulkier than untreated lining fabrics.

Interlining and Underlining

If you wish to add warmth to the coat, consider adding an interlining or an underlining during the construction. You can use either to supplement the entire coat or just parts of it. For interlining, a very loosely woven fabric such as lambswool, which traps air, is idea. It is a common practice to interline the body of the lining (and not the sleeves) by sewing the interlining pieces to the lining pieces before sewing the lining together. Another way to add warmth is to make a separate lining unit that can be zipped or buttoned into the coat when needed. This adds wearing versatility to the coat.

An underlining is used to add weight and support to the fashion fabric and at the same time it provides a little additional warmth in the finished coat. Lightweight woven interfacing or batiste are common choices for underlining.

Since adding either an interlining or underlining adds bulk to the finished garment, make sure that the coat fits with enough ease for comfort.

Interfacing

In most tailored garments, the interfacing of choice is hymo (hair canvas). Hymo is a unique woven fabric, made to retain its original form. For this reason, it is an ideal support fabric that helps to keep the coat smooth and wrinkle free. Unlike the outer fabrics, which can stretch or shrink, hymo must be sewn and molded into the desired shape because it will not stay shaped without help. In addition, hymo is unlike other fabrics because it contains a certain amount of goat hair. This causes hymo to cling to the outer fabric, helping the two layers of fabric to act as one.

Hymo is available in various fiber contents, combining wool with cotton and synthetics. Since wool is a very resilient fiber, the higher the wool content, the springier and more resistant to wrinkling and creasing the hymo will be. Hymo is also made in a wide range of weights. Choose one that complements the outer fashion fabric without overpowering it. When in doubt, select an interfacing that is lighter in weight than one that is heavier than the weight of the outer fabric.

OTHER SUPPORT FABRICS

In addition, you will need a lightweight muslin to back the hem allowances and the upper portion of the garment back in the shoulder area. For strong, durable pockets, use muslin or pocketing fabric for the inner pocket bags. Padding for the chest area is optional. A special felt-like padding fabric is available in tailoring supply stores.

COAT PATTERN PREPARATION

Commercial pattern companies use standardized allowances for fit. They use such terms as "fitted," "semi-fitted," "loosely fitted," and "very loosely fitting" to indicate the amount of wearing ease and design ease that is built into the pattern. Refer to the ease chart below. It is an adaptation of measurements used by the Vogue Pattern Company.

Compare the actual measurements of the pattern pieces with body measurements plus ease. The amount of ease depends on the styling and varies greatly. (See chart) Remember that a coat is worn over other clothing, even bulky sweaters and jackets, so the amount of ease needed for comfort must be considered when preparing the pattern.

Generally a coat should fit snugly around the neckline and shoulders and fairly loose and easy everywhere else (unless it is to be closely fitted). Before you cut out any pieces, make any pattern adjustments that you need for a good fit. (Refer to the resources listed in the bibliography on page 78 for more information on pattern adjustments and alterations.) After making the necessary adjustments, you will make additional changes to the pattern to allow for wearing ease in the lining and to perfect the pattern for the construction methods shown in this book.

BUTTON HOLE PLACEMENT

If you shortened or lengthened the pattern, adjust the buttonhole placements as needed for good proportion to each other and to the coat. Keep the buttonhole closest to the waistline where it is indicated and adjust the remaining ones that were affected by the length adjustment.

EASE ALLOWANCES
Bust Area

	Jackets	Coats
Fitted	3¾" to 4¼"	5¼" to 6¾"
	(9.5 cm to 10.7 cm)	(13.3 cm to 17 cm)
Semi-fitted	4⅜" to 5¾"	6⅞" to 8"
	(11.1 cm to 14.5 cm)	(17.4 cm to 25 cm)
Loosely fitted	5⅞" to 10"	8⅛" to 12"
	(14.8 cm to 25 cm)	20.7 cm to 30.5 cm
Very loosely fitted	10" or more	12" or more
	(25.5 cm or more)	(30.5 cm or more)

Pocket Placement

Check the pocket location and adjust if needed for a comfortable location, compatible with your arm length. See the section on pockets, beginning on page 38 for more information on pocket locations.

Upper Collar

The upper collar should be about ⅛" (3 mm) larger all around than the undercollar pattern piece to allow for the turn of cloth. Heavier fabrics may need even more of an allowance. Test by pinning a square of your fashion fabric to an identical square of paper, then fold both layers together with the paper layer inside. The amount that the fabric square draws back, exposing the paper, is the amount of allowance to add to the upper collar pattern piece.

Undercollar

The undercollar should be cut on the true bias and in two pieces to be joined in a center back seam. The collar roll line should also be indicated on the pattern tissue. For instructions on locating the roll line, see the section on fitting the coat, beginning on page 58.

Lapel

If there is a lapel, the lapel roll line should be indicated. For instructions on locating the lapel roll line, refer to page 16.

Lining

1. There should be a 1" - deep (2.5 cm) pleat at the center back, folding from right to left. Add, if not included in your pattern. See Figure 116.
2. There should be an ease tuck in the front shoulder. If not, extend the front edge as shown in Figure 116 to allow for it. Also raise the shoulder seam ⅛" (3 mm) on the front and back pattern pieces, tapering back to nothing at the neckline and extend the armhole seam ⅛" at the shoulder, tapering to nothing at the armhole notches.
3. Raise the sleeve cap and the underarm ¼" (6 mm) as shown in Figure 117.

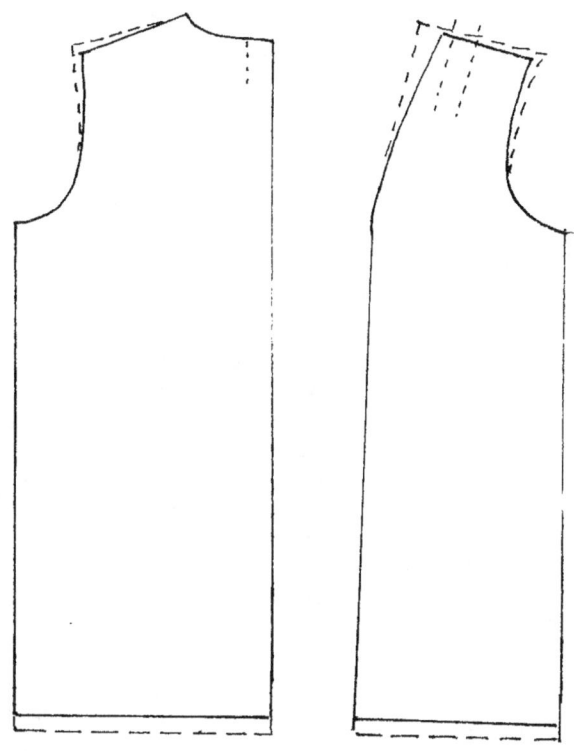

Fig 117

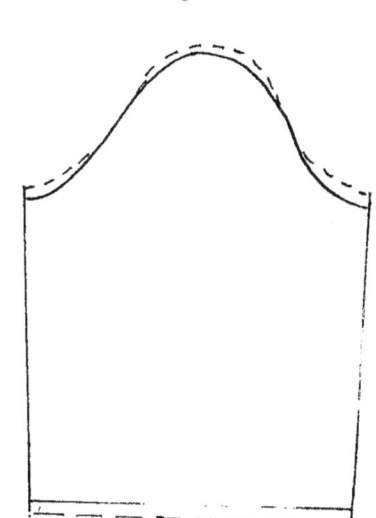

4. In most commercial patterns, the lining pattern pieces are shorter than the coat pattern pieces. Lengthen the lining pieces, including the sleeve lining, to match the coat pattern pieces. This allows enough fabric for a twice-turned hem. The lining hangs better with this added weight at the bottom.

INTERFACING

The interfacing pattern pieces provided in a commercial pattern vary from company to company; it is best to draft new interfacing pattern pieces. Use the coat front and back pattern pieces and the original front facing pattern piece to do this.

1. Place the facing pattern on top of the coat front pattern piece and draw a new cutting line for the interfacing. Extend the upper section all the way out to the armhole and curve it down under the armhole at the side seam 2½" to 3" (6.5 cm to 7.5 cm). Extend the lower half of the interfacing 1" (2.5 cm) past the inner edge of the front facing to make the interfacing wider than the facing. Trace the new interfacing pattern piece, including all existing seam allowances (Figure 118).
2. On the coat back pattern piece, draw a back stay pattern that covers the entire upper portion of the coat back, extending from the shoulder down to about 2½" to 3" (6.5 cm to 7.5 cm) below the armhole. Draw the lower edge in a gentle curve. This piece may be placed on the fold of the muslin or cut with a center back seam, depending on the pattern design.
3. If a separate pattern piece is not provided for the collar interfacing, use the undercollar pattern piece.
4. No pattern pieces are required for the hem interfacings. Cut 3"- to 4"- wide (7.5 cm to 10 cm) bias strips of muslin for this purpose.

FABRIC PREPARATION, LAYOUT AND CUTTING

Refer to the section on fabric preparation for the jacket, beginning on page 9.

1. Lay the fabric on the cutting table, folded with selvages even and parallel to the edge of the table nearest you. Pass a yardstick between the layers to separate them to make it easier to straighten the fabric.

Note: Pay special attention to plaids, stripes, diagonals, and napped fabrics. Consult the pattern guidesheet or one of the references listed in the "Bibliography" on page 74 for information on pattern layouts for these special fabrics.

2. Place all pattern pieces on the fabric following the pattern layout. Always check and recheck the layout before cutting to make sure that all required pieces are in place.
3. Chalk mark around all pieces on the fabric before cutting.
4. Cut all components of the coat at one time if possible to avoid losing a piece or cutting too many.

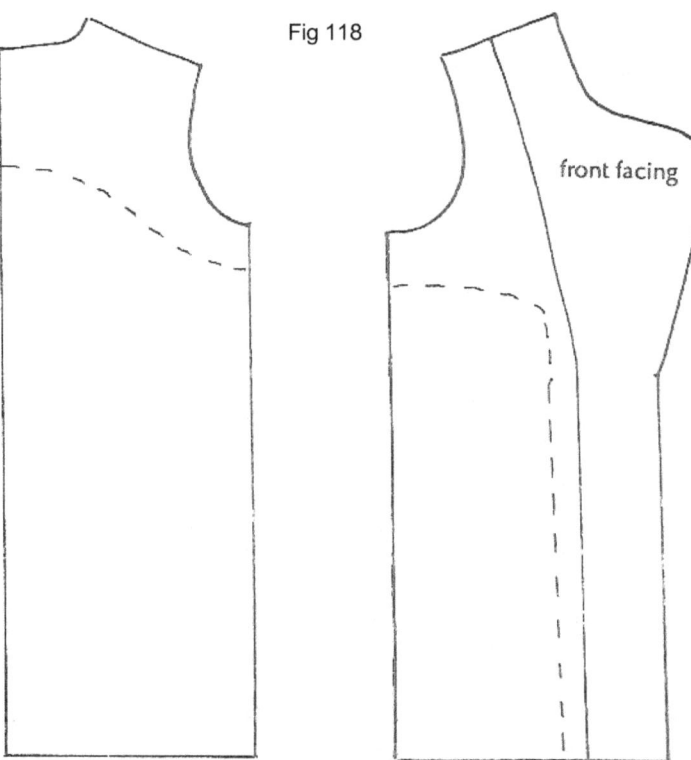

Fig 118

front facing

Marking

There are various ways to transfer markings from the pattern to the fabric and among them are "tailor tacks" and "mark stitches." Tailor tacks are typically used by seamstresses and dressmakers and mark stitches are used by tailors. Mark stitches are faster and less likely to tear the paper pattern than tailor tacks. (If you forget to cut the loops on tailor tacks, you often tear the pattern and pull out the tailor tacks.)

Note: Chalk or pencil markings are permissible on the interfacings. *Do not use tracing paper.* It leaves indelible marks on many fabrics and can show through to the right side on lightweight and light colored fashion fabrics and lining fabrics. It is difficult to use on heavier fabrics and most often results in torn pattern pieces. Thread markings are safer and can be easily removed if you make a marking error.

Mark Stitches

1. Using a length of cotton darning thread or embroidery floss, take a small stitch on the spot to be marked. Without clipping the thread, move to the next spot to be marked in the same area (Figure 119b).
2. Clip the thread that is floating between the marked spots.
3. Carefully remove the pattern.
4. Carefully separate the layers and clip the threads between them, leaving tufts of thread on both layers.
5. Trim the tufts to a scant ⅛" (3 mm) and pound with a fist to flatten the threads against the fabric.

Snip Marks

Mark notches that occur along the cut edges of the garment pieces. Make a cut into the seam allowance no longer than ³⁄₁₆" (5 mm) at each notch.

Tailor Tacks

1. Using a needle with a doubled strand of sewing thread, take a small stitch on the spot to be marked, stitching through the pattern and both layers of fabric.
2. Take another stitch in the same spot, leaving a loop (Figure 119a).
3. Clip the loops.
4. Carefully remove the pattern pieces from the cut fabric pieces.
5. Carefully separate the two layers of fabric and clip the loop threads between them, leaving tufts of thread on both layers.

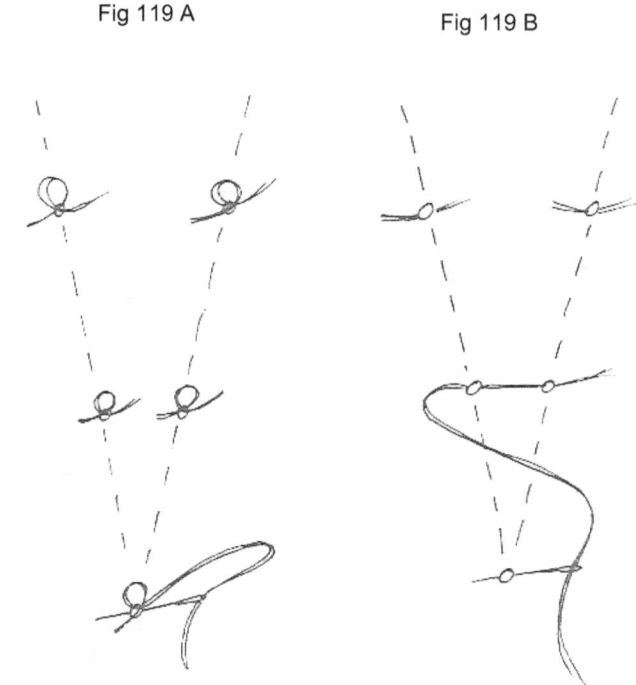

Fig 119 A   Fig 119 B

FIRST FITTING

The first fitting is probably the most important one of the several fittings needed to ensure a good-looking, well-fitting tailored coat. At this point, it is necessary to check the roll lines of the collar and lapels and the locations of pockets and buttonholes as well as the general fit and hang of the garment.

To prepare for the first fitting:
1. Stitch all darts, baste interfacings in place, and baste the main pieces of the garment together. Use short, even basting stitches and finger press the seams open for the fitting.
2. To attach the undercollar, place the right side of the undercollar on the wrong side of the garment neckline, matching notches and with seamlines on top of each other. Pin in place with pins along the seamline on the coat.
3. Beginning at the center back, baste along the seamline toward the center front, stitching through all layers. Repeat on the remaining half of the neckline.
4. Position shoulder pads and pin in place from the outside.

FIRST FITTING CHECKLIST

It is ideal to have someone help you with this, since it is difficult to make adjustments in the back. A three-way mirror is a wonderful help when fitting, with or without someone's assistance. Check the following:
1. The shoulder seam should lie squarely on the shoulder line.
2. The center front line of the right front should lie exactly on the center front line of the left front. (Reverse this for men's coats.)
3. The collar and lapels should lie smoothly and the collar should cover the neckline seam at the center back when it is in the correct position. If the roll lines of the collar and lapel were not marked on the pattern and transferred to the interfacing, and if the fit in these areas is satisfactory, pin mark the roll lines. Place pins on the roll line and parallel to it.
4. All darts should be in the correct location in relation to the body curves beneath. Check bustline darts in particular.
5. There should be enough ease through the bust, waist, and hip areas so that the coat hangs without wrinkles and is true to the design.
6. Pocket locations should be accessible to the hand without having to lift or reach unnaturally to get to the pockets. To check welt pockets, pin the welt in place and test by placing your hand over the welt as if it were tucked into the finished bag. The pocket bags should not be so far to the center that they get in the way of the buttonholes.
7. Check the buttonhole placement. Make sure there is one just slightly above the waistline and there is one where the lapel roll line crosses the front edge. Space the remaining buttonholes evenly, based on the number required.
8. Check the lapel roll line for gapping. If it gaps, pin out a tuck to indicate how much excess there is.
9. Mark any required alterations with chalk or basting stitches.
10. Take the coat apart to facilitate working on details such as pockets and buttonholes.

BUTTONHOLES AND POCKETS

If you plan to make bound buttonholes, do so now. Otherwise, make machine buttonholes after the coat is completed. There are a number of different methods for making bound buttonholes. Choose a method from one of the tailoring references listed in the Bibliography on page 74. Be sure to make a few practice buttonholes in scraps of the coat fabric before making them in the coat front.

If your coat has vertical welt pockets, refer to the directions on page 70. For patch pockets, see pages 26 and 42.

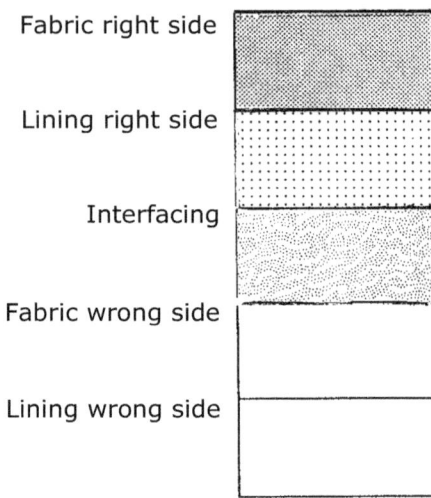

Fabric right side

Lining right side

Interfacing

Fabric wrong side

Lining wrong side

Interfacing Preparation

Darts

There are two methods for making darts in the hymo hair canvas interfacing. Both eliminate bulk in this stiffer interfacing.

Method One
1. Cut out the dart on the marked stitching line (Figure 120).
2. Butt the cut edges and tuck a narrow strip of fusible interfacing underneath. Fuse to secure. Or, tuck a strip of lining fabric under the dart and stitch in place to hold the cut edges in place (Figure 120).Method

Method Two
1. Slash through the center of the dart (Figure 121).
2. Lap the dart with stitching lines on top of each other and stitch (Figure 121).

Applying Edge Tape and Padstitching the Interfacing

1. Mark the roll line on the front interfacing pieces with chalk or pencil. From the break point at the bottom of the lapel roll line to the hem, draw a guide line ⅞" (2.2 cm) from and parallel to the front cut edge (Figure 122).
2. Cut a piece of ⅜"-wide (1 cm) preshrunk edge tape a little longer than the distance from the bottom edge of the coat, up along the lapel edge to the roll line. Place one edge along the line just drawn with approximately ½" (1.3 cm) of the hymn showing along the cut edge (Figure 123).
3. Machine stitch the inside edge (toward the side seam) to the hymo from the hem to the breakpoint. Leave enough tape to reach to the neck edge along the edge and cut away excess. You will stitch this in place later (Figure 124).

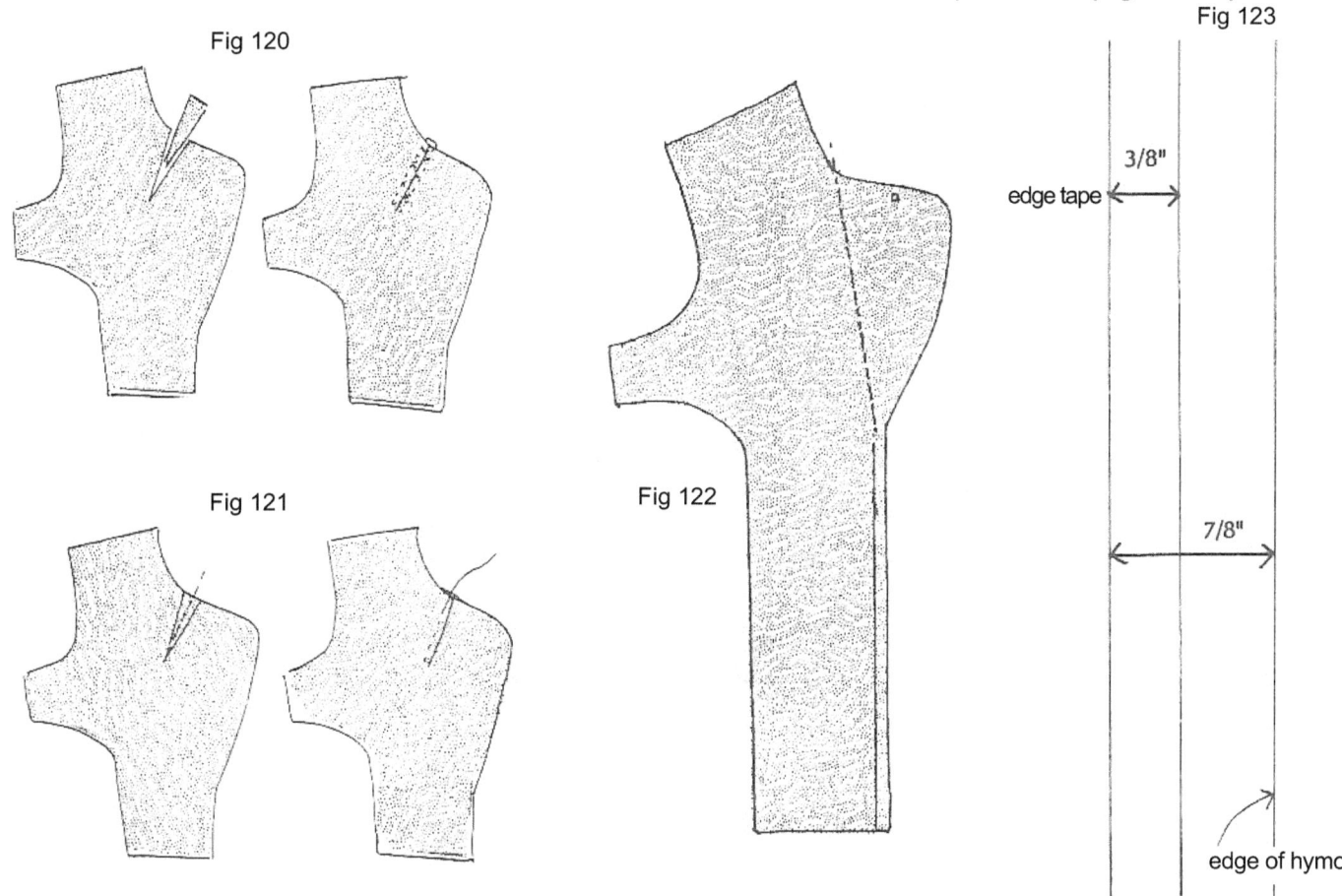

Fig 120

Fig 121

Fig 122

Fig 123

Interfacing Application

Applying Hymo to the Coat Front

1. Place the prepared front interfacing on the table with the taped side down.
2. Lay the coat front right side up on top of the hymo, with the cut edges of both layers even.
3. Baste the layers together along the lapel roll line with a running stitch. Use large diagonal basting stitches to hold the hymo in place outside the lapel area. *Do not baste inside the seam allowances.* Make three rows of basting as shown in Figure 125.

    As you baste, run your hand down the front of the coat to smooth the fabric and to keep it slightly taut. This helps eliminate bubbles and ripples on the front of the garment (Figure 126).

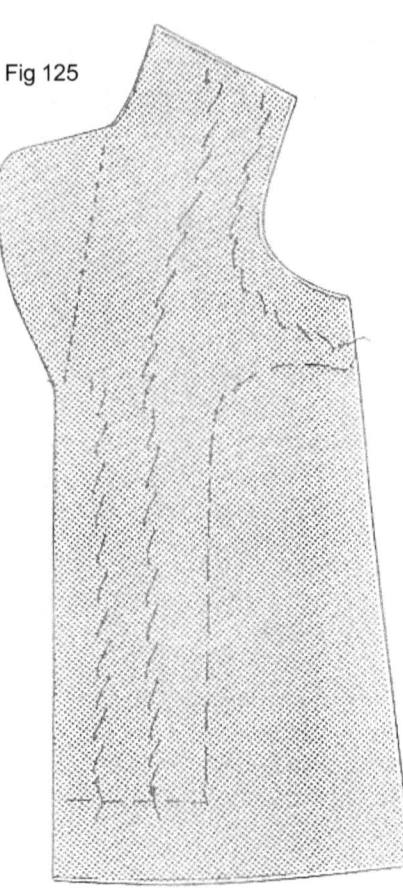

Fig 125

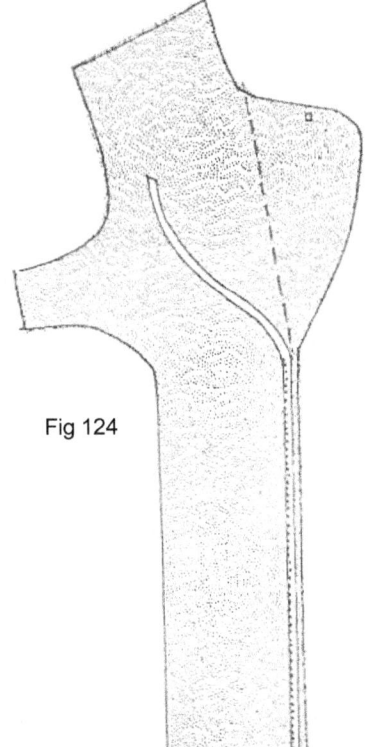

Fig 124

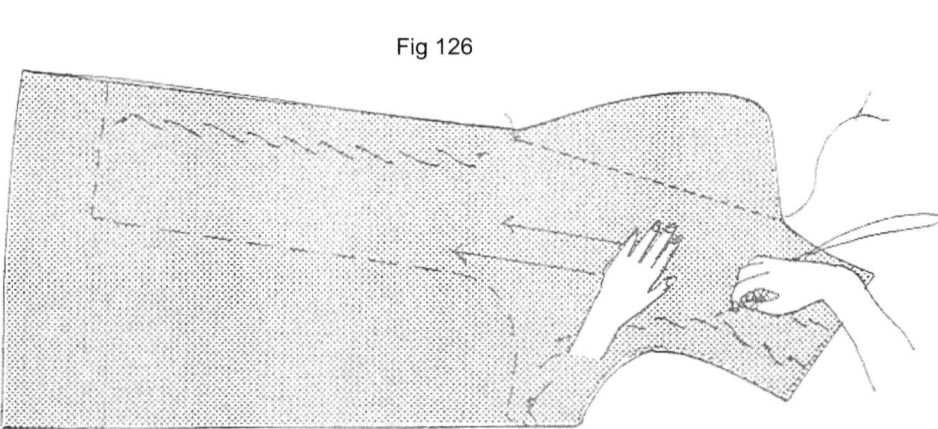

Fig 126

Pad Stitching the Hymo

1. Place the right and left coat fronts on the table with the interfacing side up. Check to make sure they are identical in size and shape.

2. Place a piece of ⅜"-wide (1 cm) preshrunk edge tape parallel to and ¼" (6 mm) away from the lapel roll line (toward the armhole, not toward the lapel). Start the tape at the neckline seam line and end 2" (5 cm) above the top button location. Cut to fit this length. Baste into position, shortening if necessary to eliminate the excess gap in the roll line you marked during the first fitting. You can cut off as much as ½" (1.3 cm) of the tape. Pin the top end of the tape in place at the neckline, then pin the bottom end in place 2" (5 cm) above the button location and ease the roll line onto the tape. Center the ease in the middle third of the roll line. This helps the roll line hug the bustline curve and eliminates gapping along the roll line (Figure 127).

3. Using thread that matches the coat fabric, fell stitch each edge of the tape to the hymo, catching only a thread or two of the coat fabric underneath in each stitch (Figure 128).

4. Turn the fronts over so they are right side up. Lift the hymo away from the coat in the lapel area, then roll the lapel into the finished position. The lapel of the coat will extend a bit beyond the outer edge of the interfacing in the lapel area (Figure 129).

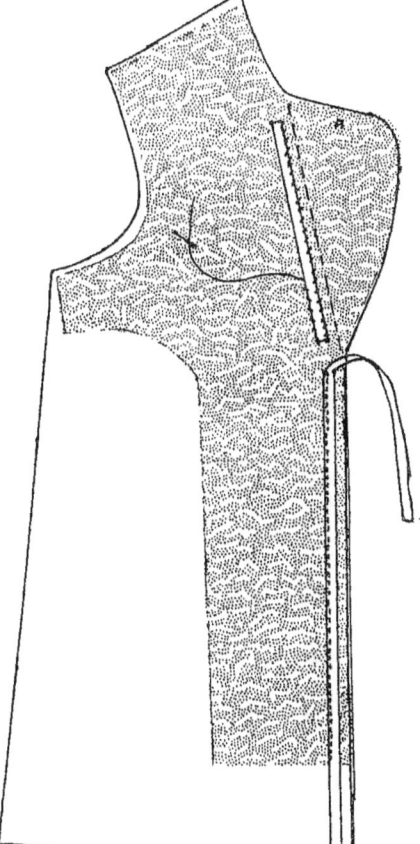

Fig 127

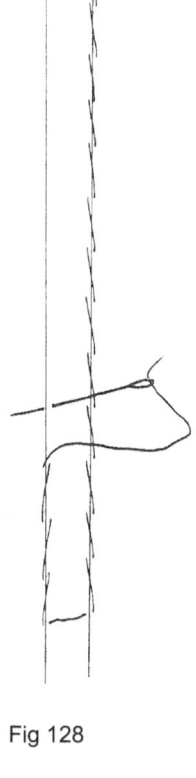

Fig 128

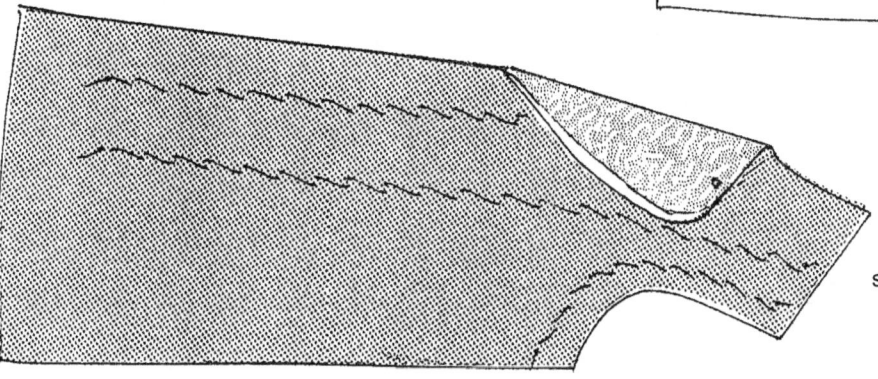

Fig 129

separate layers in lapel area

5. Pad stitch the roll line in the rolled position (Figure 130).

6. Using thread to match the coat fabric, pad stitch the lapel, covering the entire area except the seam allowances (Figure 131). Space rows of pad stitches ½" apart. Work from the roll line out to the front edge, taking ⅛"-long stitches that just barely catch the fashion fabric. As you stitch, push *very slightly* with your thumb on the hymo and *gently* curl the lapel points in toward the body of the garment. Stitch the first row working toward you, then do the second in the opposite direction. Stagger the rows of stitches as shown in Figure 132a rather than lining them up as shown in Figure 132b. Staggering the rows prevents ridges forming in the interfacing.

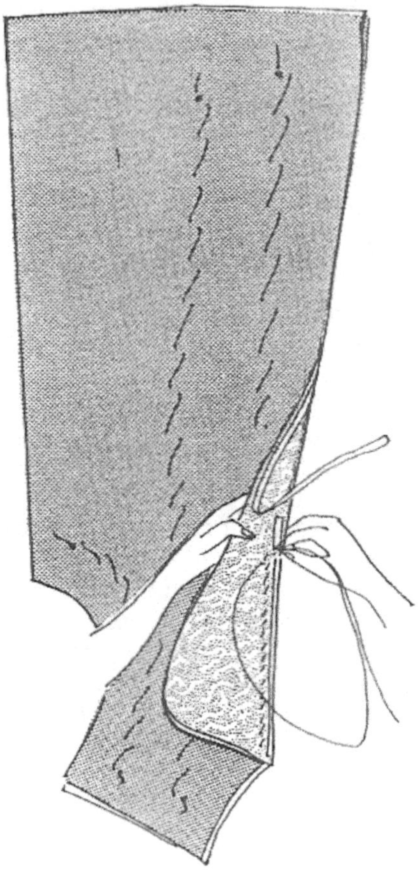

Fig 130
pad stitch roll line

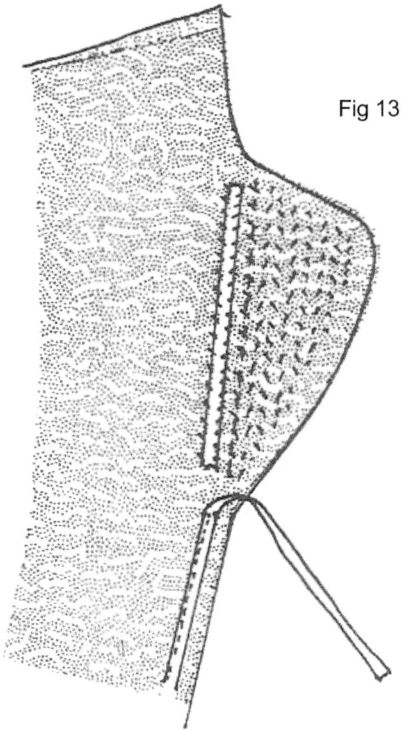

Fig 131

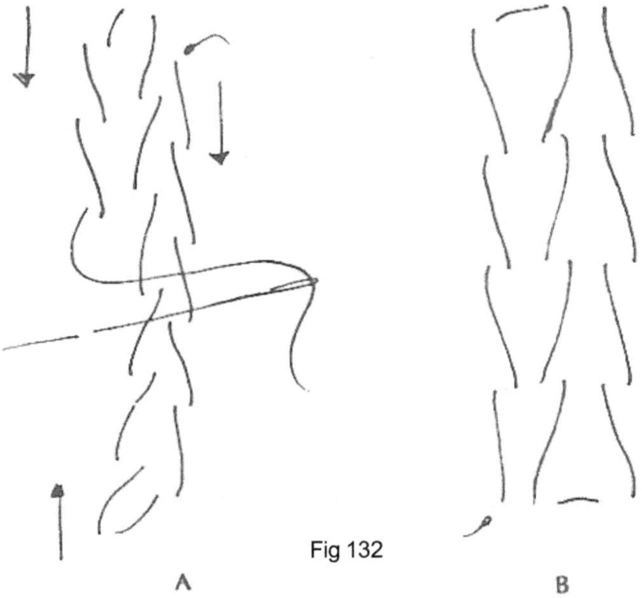

Fig 132
A   B

Attaching Edge Tape

1. Trim away the hymo along the front edges from the collar notch to the hem. Cut ⅛" (3 mm) inside the seam allowance, being careful not to cut the coat fabric as you trim the interfacing away. Also trim away the hymo along the neckline to the shoulder (Figure 133).

2. After trimming, the edge tape should overlap the cut edge of the interfacing about ⅛" (3 mm) so that it will be caught in the stitching along the seam line. Baste the outer edge of the tape to the coat front seam allowance. At the lapel breakpoint, baste the tape with a tiny bit of ease in it to relieve the strain of the roll at that point.

3. Continue basting the tape over the cut edge of the interfacing in the lapel area and around the lapel, ending at the collar termination point. To apply around curves, slash the inner edges of the tape and overlap. *Do not slash the outer edge of the tape as that will weaken it.* Then fell stitch the inner edge of the tape to the hymo and the outer edge of the tape to the seam allowance (Figure 134).

4. Stitch the outer edge of the tape to the seam allowance from the break point down to the bottom edge. Do this by hand with a fell stitch or carefully stitch by machine when you are actually sewing the front facing to the coat.

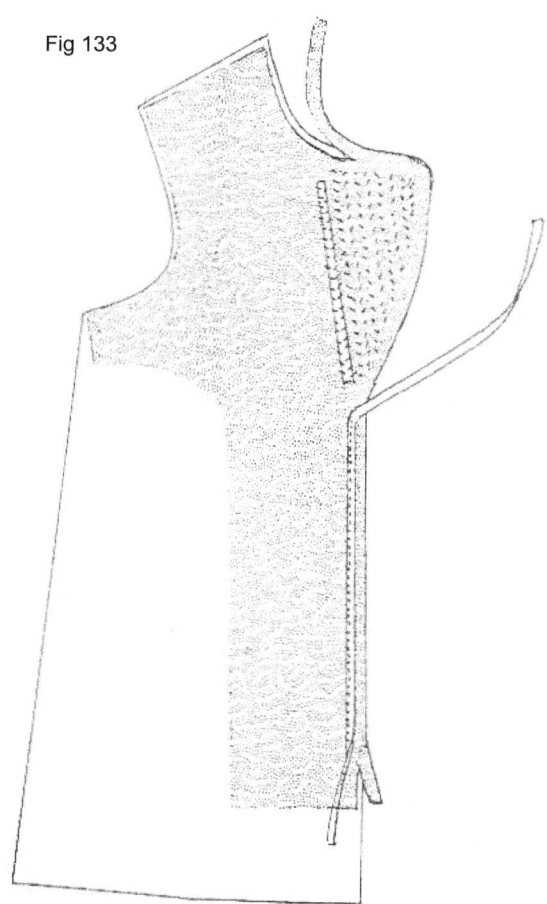

Fig 133

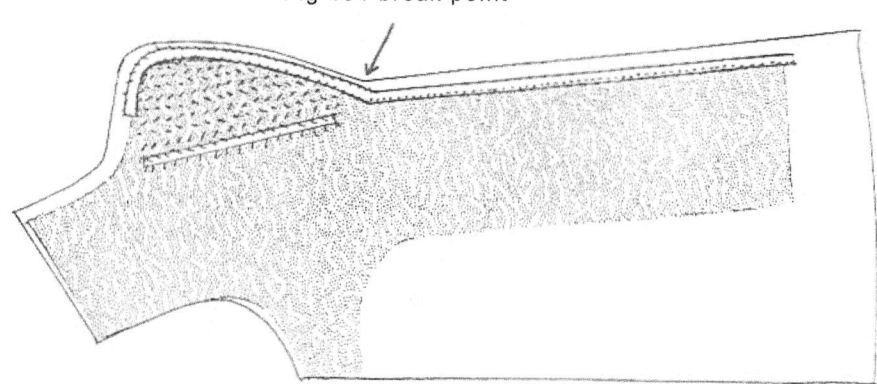

Fig 134 break point

Applying the Back Interfacing

The upper back of the coat requires interfacing for support across the shoulders and into the underarm areas.

1. Most coat patterns allow for a dart in the back shoulder area. If the coat fabric is not too thick and heavy, it is better to convert the dart to ease. Easestitch along the entire length of the shoulder seam and draw up the stitching so the back shoulder seam matches the front shoulder seam. Adjust the ease so most of it is centered in the back shoulder seam as shown in Figure 135.

2. Carefully steam out the fullness.
3. To help stabilize the shoulder seam, fuse a narrow strip of interfacing or edge tape to the back shoulder seam allowance after steaming out the ease.
4. Prepare the back interfacing by stitching darts and the center back seam (if there is one).
5. Position the interfacing on the wrong side of the coat back, keeping all raw edges even. Pin in place around the outer edges. Then with the coat back face up, place a pressing ham under the dart area and baste the two layers together with large diagonal stitches (Figure 136).

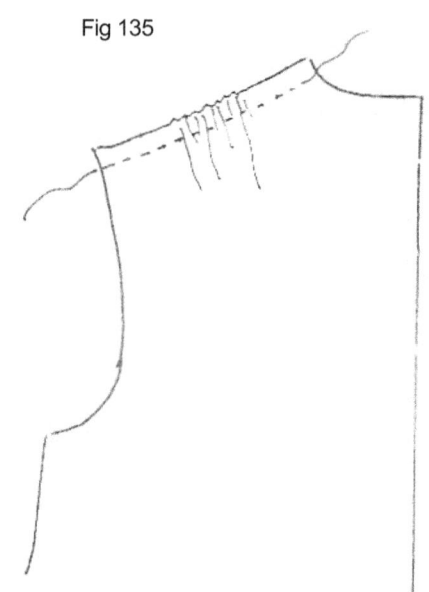

Fig 135

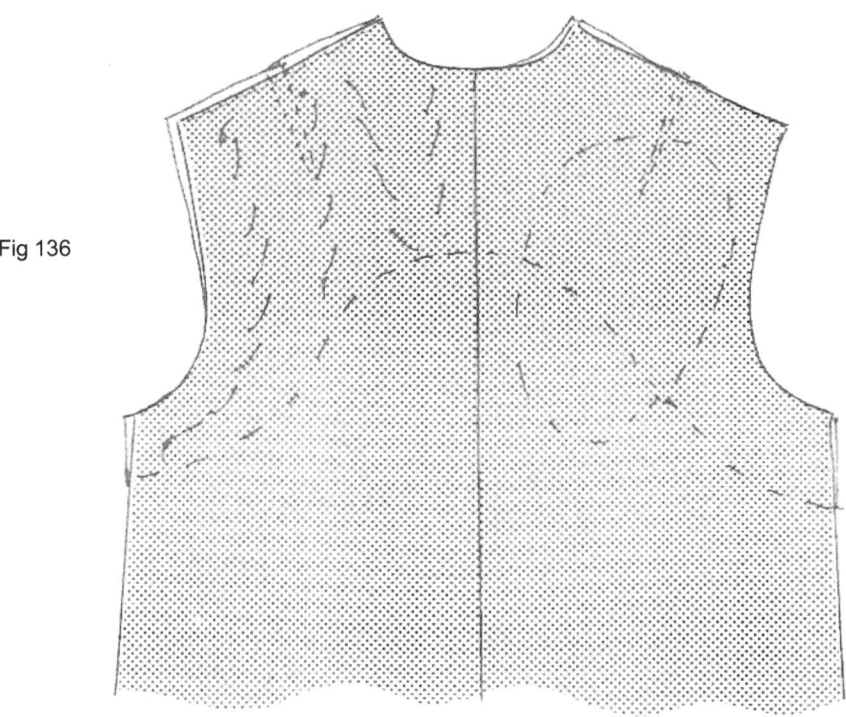

Fig 136

Interfacing The Collar

1. With right sides together, stitch the center back seam of the undercollar. Trim the seam to ¼" (6mm) and press open.
2. Overlap the center back seamlines of the undercollar interfacing pieces and machine stitch together on the seamline.
3. Place the interfacing on the wrong side of the undercollar, aligning the center back seams. Machine stitch together on the roll line. (Figure 137).
4. Fill the stand area of the collar with short and closely stitched padstitching, catching only a thread or two of the collar fabric in the stitching. Shape the collar over your hand as you pad stitch (Figure 138). *Do not padstitch within the seam allowances.*
5. Fill in the fall area of the collar using slightly longer and less densely spaced padstitching; shape and push slightly with the thumb as you stitch to help keep the roll in the collar (Figure 139). *Do not padstitch within the seam allowances.*
6. Carefully trim away the interfacing seam allowances and catchstitch the trimmed edges of the interfacing to the seamline of the undercollar.
7. Pin the padstitched undercollar to a tailor's ham. To set the shape, steam press along the roll line (Figure 140). Leave the undercollar pinned to the ham until thoroughly dry.

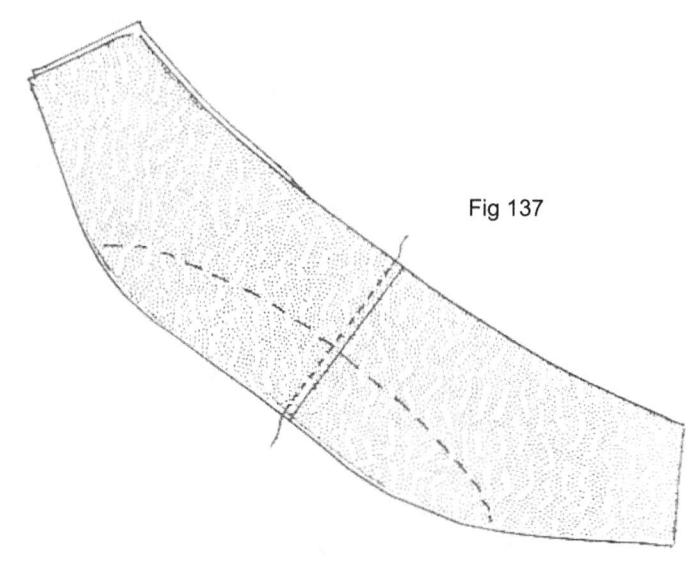

Fig 137

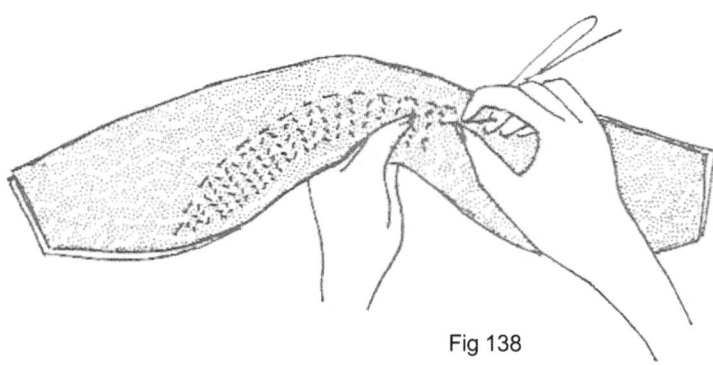

Fig 138

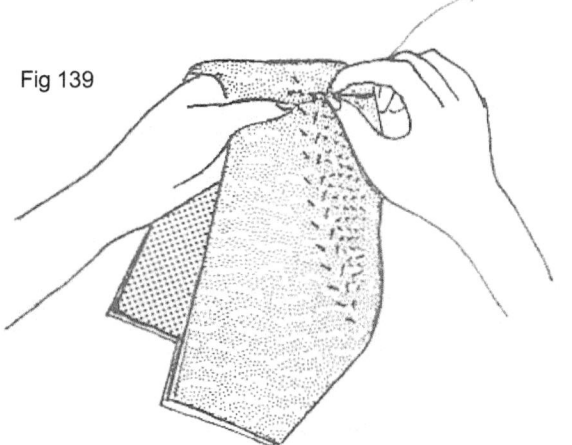

Fig 139

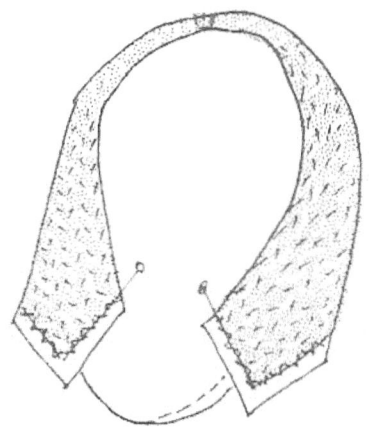

Fig 140

Attaching the Undercollar

1. Stitch the coat fronts to the back at the shoulder seams. Press the seam open.
2. Lay the shoulder edge of the front interfacing over the pressed seam and catchstitch to the neckline seam allowance and to shoulder seam (Figure 141).
3. With right sides together, pin the undercollar to the coat neckline. Clip the neckline seam allowance as needed to make collar fit smoothly. With the clipped neckline on top, stitch the neckline seam, being careful to begin and end at the seamline, not at the cut edge of the undercollar. (See the arrows in Figure 142.)
4. Trim the neckline seam allowance of the coat and the collar to ⅜" (1 cm) and press the seam open over a tailor's ham.

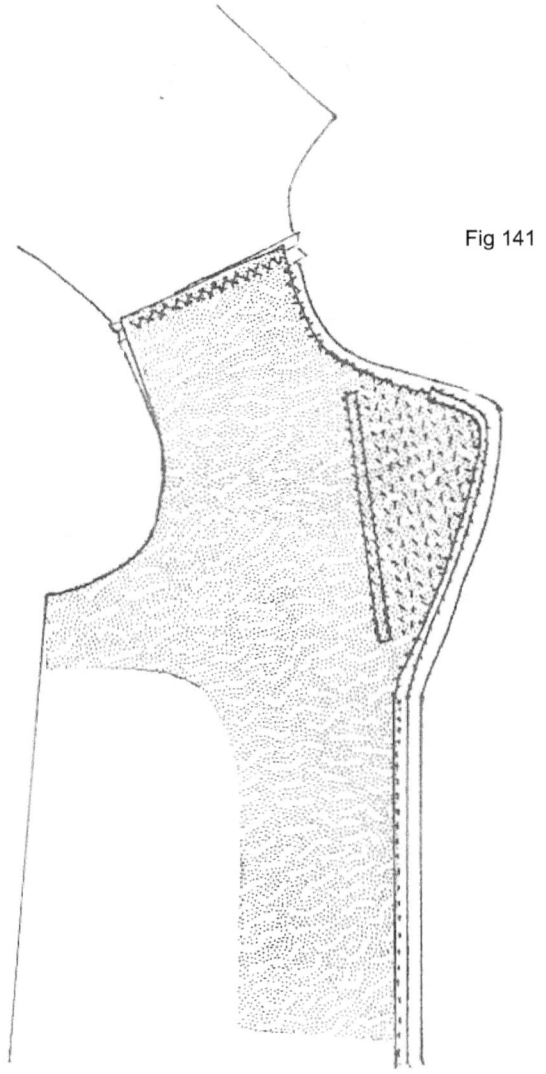

Fig 141

Fig 142

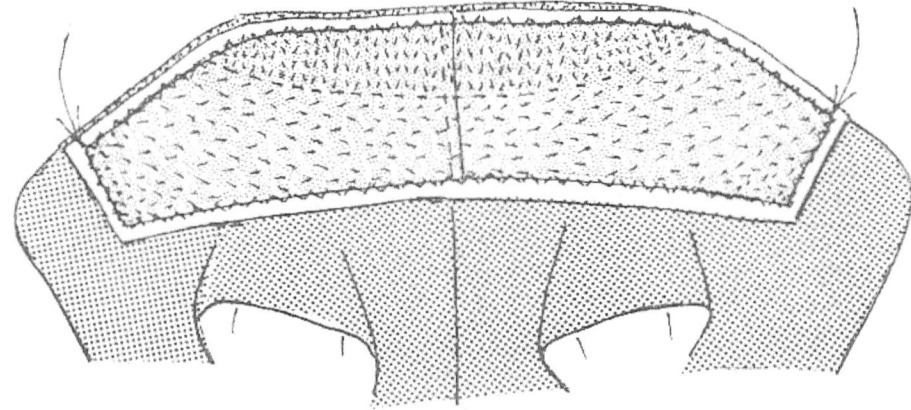

Sleeve Assembly and Insertion

1. Position a 4"-wide (10 cm) bias strip of muslin on the wrong side of each sleeve, with the lower edge of the strip about ⅝" (1.5 cm) below the actual hemline. Blind stitch along the hemline and the upper edge. Stitch the ends of the strip to the seam allowances (Figure 143).
2. Ease the cap of the sleeve using one of the following methods:
a. Do two rows of easestitching, then draw up so the sleeve fits into the armhole (Figure 144).
b. Incorporate a header into the cap while doing the easestitching shown above to shorten the cap line. Do this by anchoring a 4"-wide (10 cm) bias strip of muslin, folded in half lengthwise, to the seam near the armhole notch(es) on one side of the sleeve. Then stretch the muslin as you sew it to the sleeve cap while easestitching (Figures 145 and 146). The header keeps the ease in place where it is needed.
3. Stitch the underarm seam and press the seam open over a sleeve board.
4. Steam out the ease in the sleeve cap so that there are no wrinkles or puckers in the cap.
5. Stitch the coat side seams and press the seams open.
6. Matching the notches, pin the sleeves into the armholes. Baste.
7. Pin a set of shoulder pads in place inside the coat. Try coat on a dress form to check the hang of the sleeves, the sleeve length, the set of the collar, roll of the lapel, and the general overall fit. Make any necessary adjustments.
8. When satisfied with the fit and appearance, permanently stitch the sleeves into the armholes. Turn up and press the sleeve hems and catchstitch the upper edge of the hem allowance to the strip of muslin interfacing.

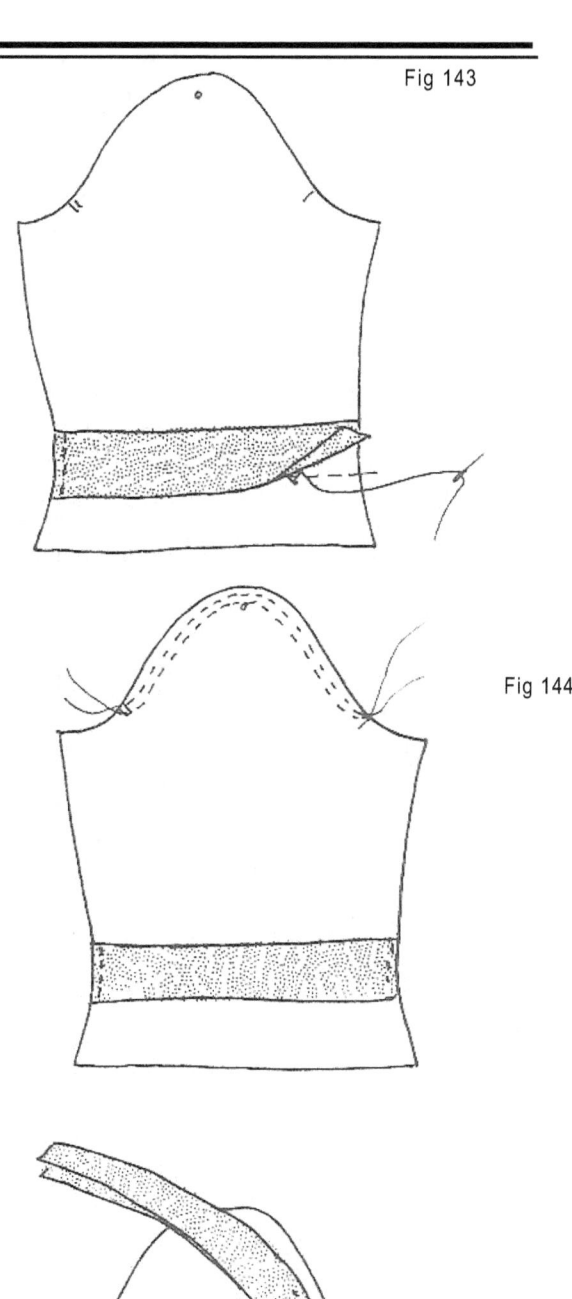

Fig 143

Fig 144

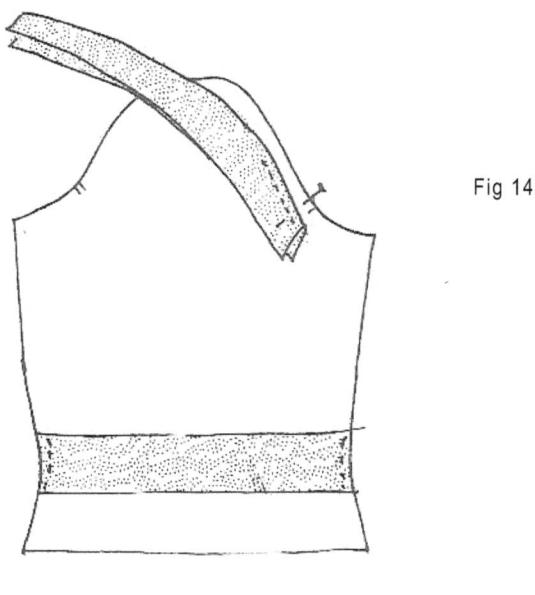

Fig 145

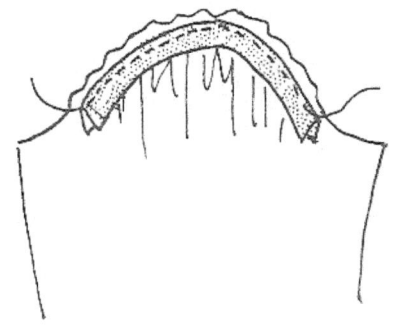

Fig 146

Assembling the Lining

First sew the front lining to the coat front facing, adding an inside pocket in the seam, following the steps below. Then complete the lining assembly.

Note: The opening for an inside coat pocket should be in the chest area with the pocket bag resting in the hollow below the breast. Measure down about 9" (23 cm) from the shoulder seam of the front facing and mark a notch for the top of the pocket opening. Then measure down an additional 5"-6" (12.8 cm-15.3 cm) and mark another notch for the bottom of the pocket opening. Make corresponding notches on the front lining (Figure 147).

1. Cut two pocket bags from the lining fabric. A pocket bag pattern is provided in back of book.
2. With right sides together, sew one of the pocket bags to the front facing at the notches you marked earlier (Figure 147). Press the seam toward the pocket (Figure 148).
3. With right sides together, sew the remaining pocket bag to the front lining at the marked location. Clip, turn the pocket to the inside and press (Figure 148).

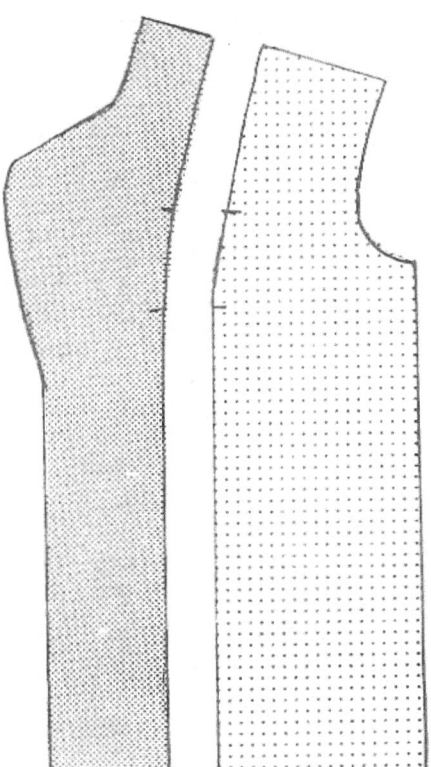

Fig 147

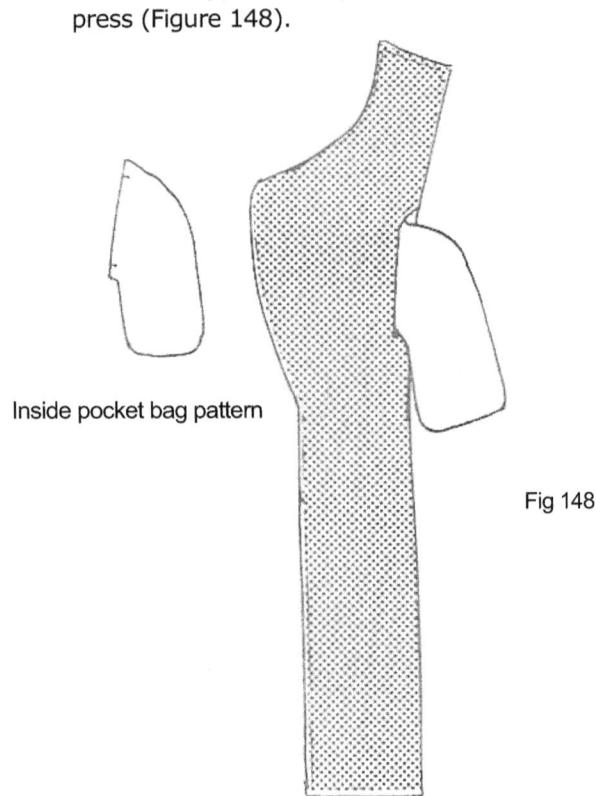

Inside pocket bag pattern

Fig 148

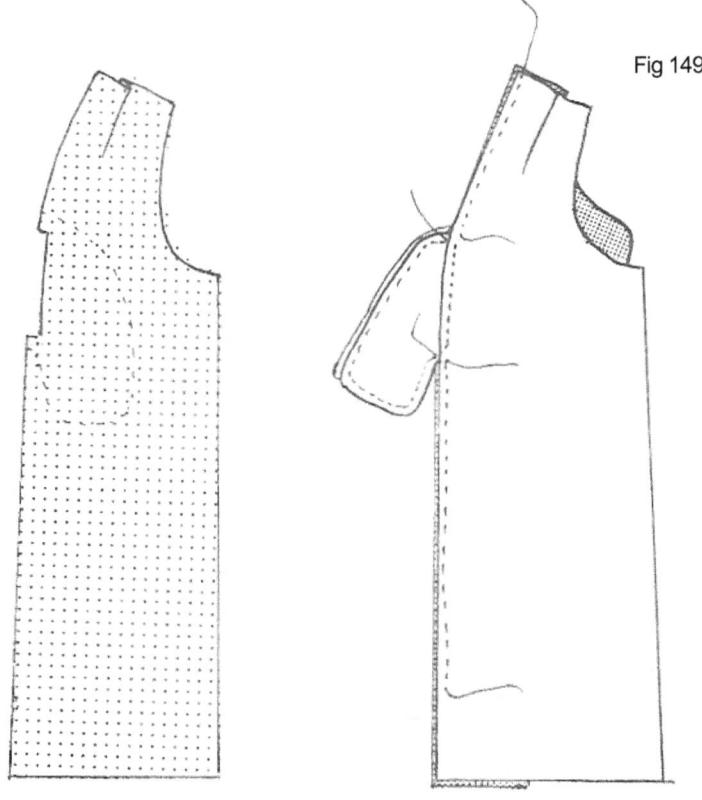

Fig 149

4. With right sides together, pin the front lining to the front facing, matching the raw edges of the pocket bags. Stitch from the shoulder down to the bag and backstitch. Break the stitching. Next sew around the bag and backstitch. Break the stitching. Continue stitching the facing to the lining, ending within 4" (10 cm) of the bottom edge. Leave the remaining seam to be finished after hemming the coat and the lining (Figure 149).

5. if there is a center back seam in the lining, stitch as directed in your pattern. To make the center back pleat, start at the neckline and stitch on the center back line for about 2" (5 cm), then pivot and angle toward the cut edges. Stitch to within ⅝" (1.5 cm), pivot again and continue stitching to the bottom, using the ⅝" (1.5 cm) seam allowance width. Press the pleat toward the left back (Figure 1 50).

6. Sew the lining front / facing units to the lining back at the shoulder and side seams. Press seams toward the back lining.

7. Easestitch around the lining sleeve caps. Stitch the sleeve underarm seams and press open.

8. Draw up the ease and pin the sleeves into the lining armholes. Match notches and adjust ease evenly. Stitch in place.

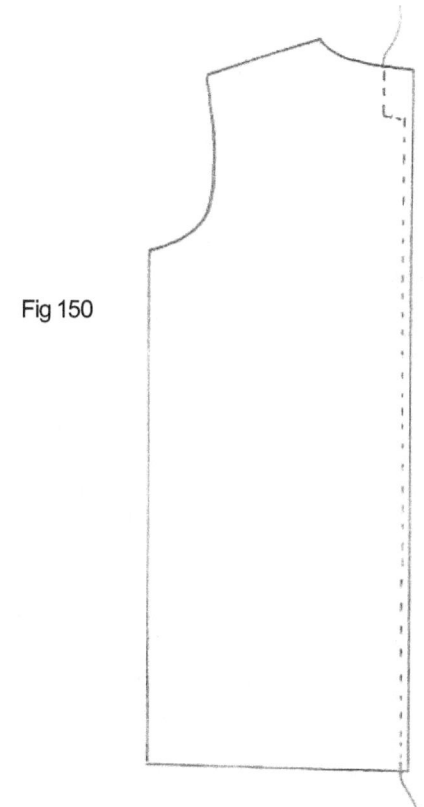

Fig 150

Attaching the Upper Collar to the Facing

1. Staystitch the neckline of the lining/facing unit to stabilize it and to make it easier to sew the upper collar in place (Figure 151).

2. With right sides together and notches matching, pin the upper collar to the facing, clipping the neckline seam allowance as needed for a smooth, pucker-free fit. Stitch from the clipped neckline side, being careful to begin and end the stitching at the seamlines, not in the seam allowances of the collar as shown in Figure 152.

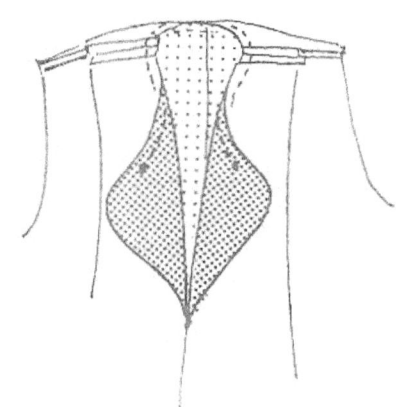

Fig 151

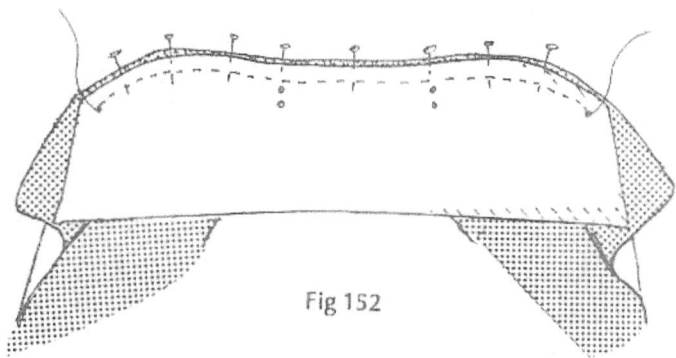

Fig 152

Sewing the Lining / Facing Unit to the Coat

1. Pin the upper collar to the undercollar, easing the upper collar to fit, especially at the collar points.
2. Using thread that matches the fashion fabric, catch the seam allowances of both collars and the lapel at the juncture where they meet and tie securely. See Figure 59, on page 30.
3. Pin the facing to coat fronts, building in a little ease at the lapel point. Also allow ease in the facing where the lapel turns back at the bottom of the roll line to ease the strain of the roll.
4. Make a paper pattern of the collar point and the lapel point. Use it to chalk in the sewing lines on the garment pieces to make sure that both sides will match after stitching.
5. Stitch the collars together, starting at the center back and stitching toward the lapel. Do not catch the upper or undercollar seam allowances in the stitching at the collar termination point. Turn them down and out of the way as shown in Figure 153.
6. Stitch the facing to the body of the coat, starting at the collar termination points, and turning the lapel seam allowances up out of the way to avoid catching them in the stitching.
7. Press all seam allowances open, using an edge board and point presser to get into the corners. If the fabric is very heavy and bulky, kill the seams before pressing them open. *To kill a seam, place the seam allowance on a wooden surface and wet the seam allowance only. Press the wet area with a hot, heavy iron. The treated area will lose all of its life and become limp and very flat.*
8. Trim seams to ⅜" (1 cm), then grade. Grade the collar seam allowances so that the upper collar seam allowance is wider than the undercollar seam allowance. Taper across the corners. Grade the lapel seam allowances so that facing seam allowance is wider. From the lapel to the bottom edge, grade so that the garment seam allowance is wider than the facing.
9. Turn the facing and collar right side out.
   Note: To anchor the seam allowances along the front edges and around the collar, use understitching or topstitching. Understitch now. Topstitch after turning the hem and completing the coat.
10. Roll the seamline of the collar and lapel edges toward the undercollar and the garment. Baste with diagonal basting stitches to hold the edges in place.
11. Roll the seam along the lower front edge toward the facing and baste with diagonal stitches to hold the edges in place.
12. Press the basted edges from the underside and use a clapper if edges require further flattening.
13. Roll the collar and lapels into their completed position and pin. Baste along the lapel and collar roll lines through all layers to hold them in place while you complete the coat.
14. Lift the lining up to expose the neckline seam and permanently baste the seam allowances of the facing and garment necklines together. *Do not do this until you have completed step 13 above.*
15. Insert the shoulder pads, anchoring the outer edge of the pad to the armhole seam allowance with a loose running stitch. Tack the pad to the shoulder seam near the neckline (Figure 154).

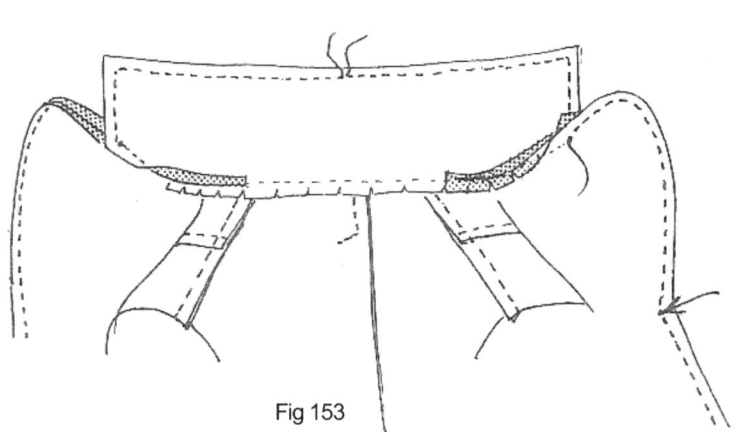

Fig 153

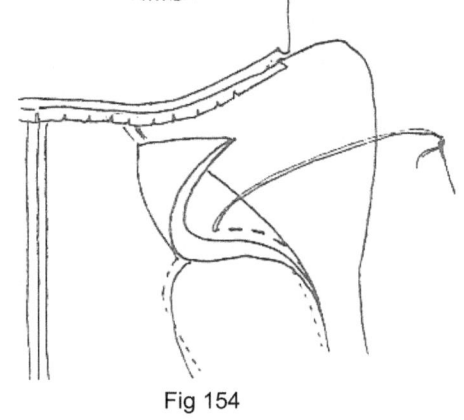

Fig 154

Hemming the Coat and the Lining

1. Interface the coat hem by placing a 4"-wide (10 cm) bias strip of muslin on the wrong side of the coat with the bottom edge about ⅝" (1.5 cm) below the intended hemline. Baste into place, overlapping about ¾" (2 cm) of the muslin strip onto the hymo interfacing in the coat front. Catchstitch together as shown in Figure 155. Anchor the muslin strip to every seam allowance with catch stitches.

   Blindstitch the muslin to the coat along the top edge and at the hemline as shown.
2. Turn up the coat hem and press. Catchstitch the top edge of the coat hem to the muslin strip. Hem the upper edge of the hem in the coat facing to the facing (Figure 156).
3. Twice turn the lining hem, making the lining about ¾" (2 cm) shorter than the coat. Slipstitch in place (Figure 156).

Securing the Loose Ends

1. With the facing laying in the desired finished position on the coat front, pin along the entire length of the facing/lining seam to attach it to the coat front (Figure 157).

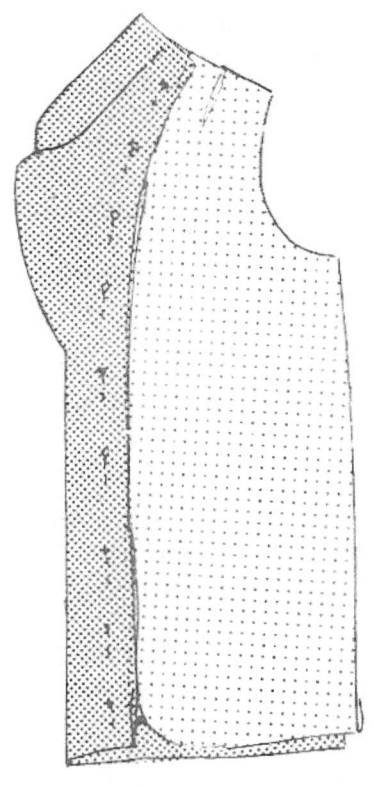

Fig 157

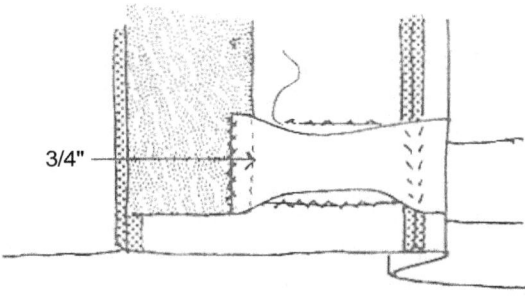

Fig 155

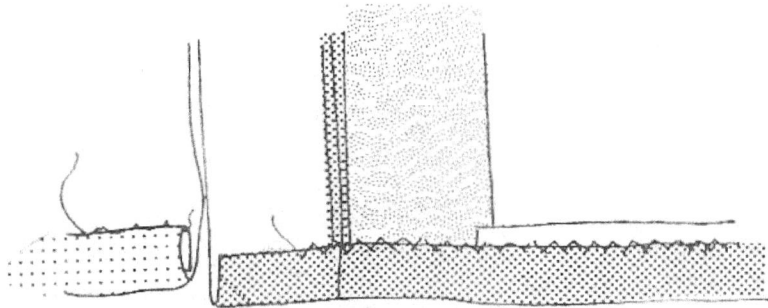

Fig 156

2. Lift up the lining and attach the seam allowance to the hymo with a running stitch. At the lower edge, catchstitch the facing edge to the hem allowance (Figure 158).
3. Slipstitch the remaining unstitched portion of the lining hem to the facing (Figure 159).
4. Beginning at the armhole attach the lining side seams to the coat side seams with a long running stitch, ending about pocket level.
5. Tack the lining armhole to the shoulder pads to keep the lining in place.
6. Secure the lining hem to the coat hem at the side seams with swing tacks (Figure 160).
7. Reach in between the coat and lining hems to draw out the sleeve and sleeve lining (both turned with wrong side out). Tack the underarm seams of both sleeves together from the armscye to the elbow area (Figure 161).
8. Slip the sleeve lining over the coat sleeve (Figure 162).
9. Turn up the bottom edge of the sleeve lining. About ¾" (2 cm) of the coat sleeve hem should show below the fold of the lining. Peel back the lining fold and slipstitch the lining to the coat hem allowance (Figure 162). When the lining is allowed to drop to its original position, an ease pleat will form.

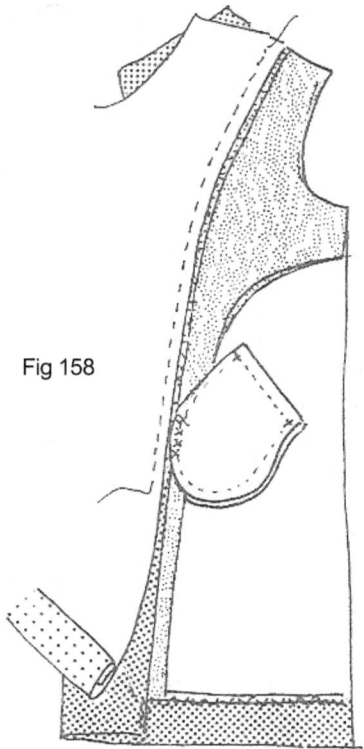

Fig 158

FINISHING

1. Topstitch around the front edges and collar if desired. Break the stitching at the turn of the lapel so that you are always stitching from the side of the coat that will be seen when worn. Hide thread ends by using a needle to draw them between the garment and facing layers (Figure 163).
2. Make machine buttonholes now, unless you made bound buttonholes earlier. if so, finish the backs by slitting the facing behind each one, then turning under and whipstitching the edges to the buttonhole welts along the stitching lines.
3. Sew the buttons in place.
4. Do a final touch-up pressing to give the garment a finished look. If you know and trust an excellent dry cleaner in your area, this is a job you may wish to ask him to do instead.

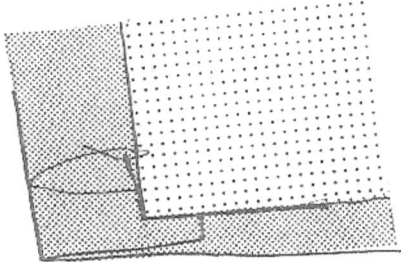

Fig 159

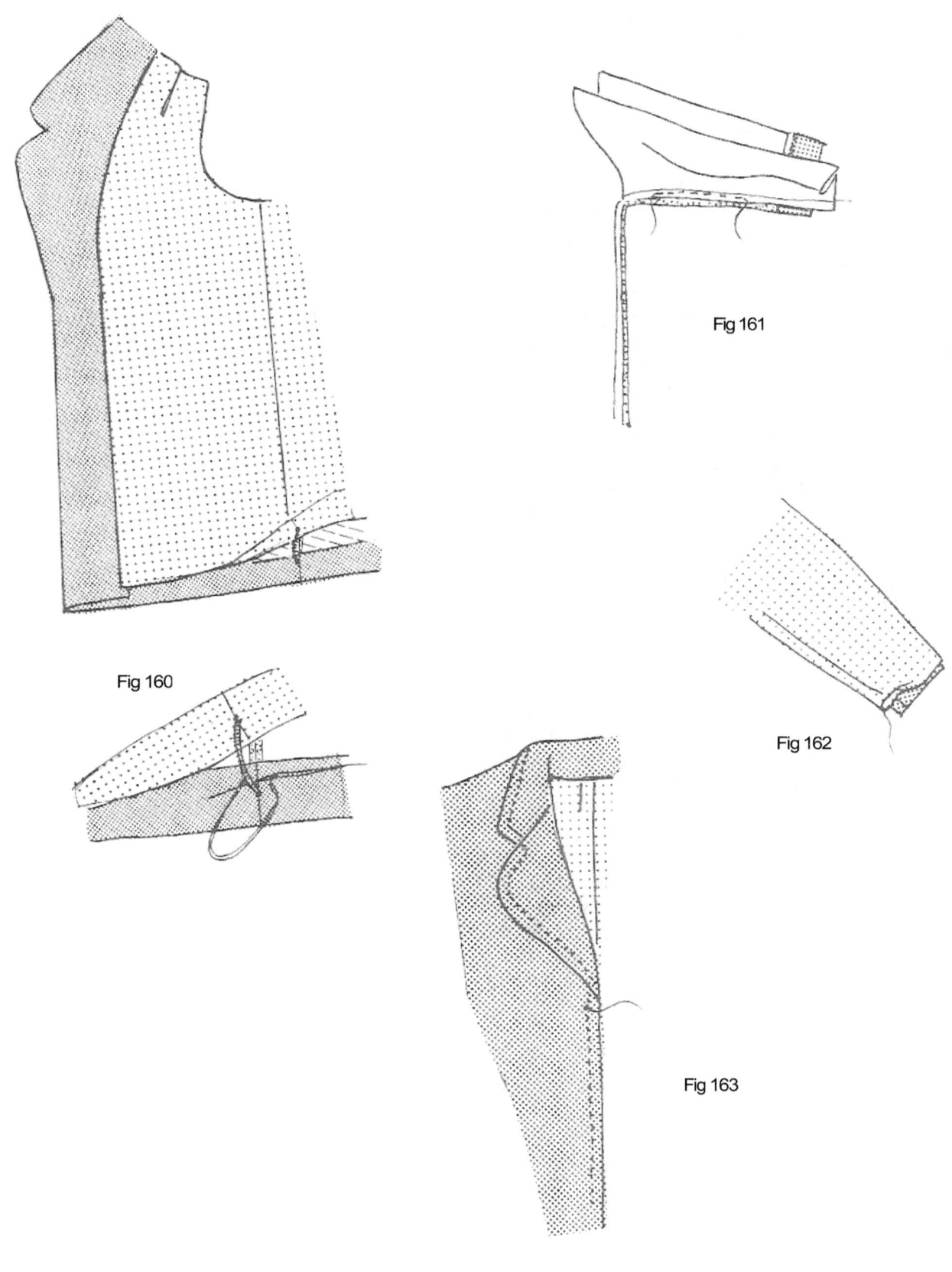

Fig 160

Fig 161

Fig 162

Fig 163

Coat Pocket

Vertical Welt Pocket

The vertical welt pocket is most commonly used in coats. In women's coats the welt is 7" to 7½" (17.7 cm to 19 cm) long and 1" to 2" (2.5 cm to 5 cm) wide. Men's welts are generally 8" to 8½" (20 cm to 21.5 cm) long and 2" (5 cm) wide.

While coat patterns usually include a welt pocket piece, I recommend redrafting the welt as shown below. For practical purposes, coat fabrics are heavier and bulkier than suitings. This creates a challenge when dealing with the enclosed seams commonly found in pocket welts. Past experiences following commercial pattern directions for making welt pockets on coats have often left me in tears. The problem is dealing with the ridge created by the seam allowances around the outer edges of the welt and the seam holding the welt to the coat. The normal manner of design and construction make it almost impossible to stitch down the triangles in the corners after slashing and turning the welt through to the right side.

Taking a cue from tailors, who always stress the importance of reducing bulk wherever possible, I adapted their method of constructing and applying welts. The method involves making a new pattern piece for the welt to create mitered corners that are completely hidden on the underside of the welt (Figure 164). Pattern pieces made using this technique are given in the back of the book, but you should know how to draft this shape for a welt of any size. The most common shapes, along with an illustration of the corresponding new pattern pieces, are shown in Figure 164. The straight welt is shown and described in the following steps. The angled welt requires some modification in folding and marking.

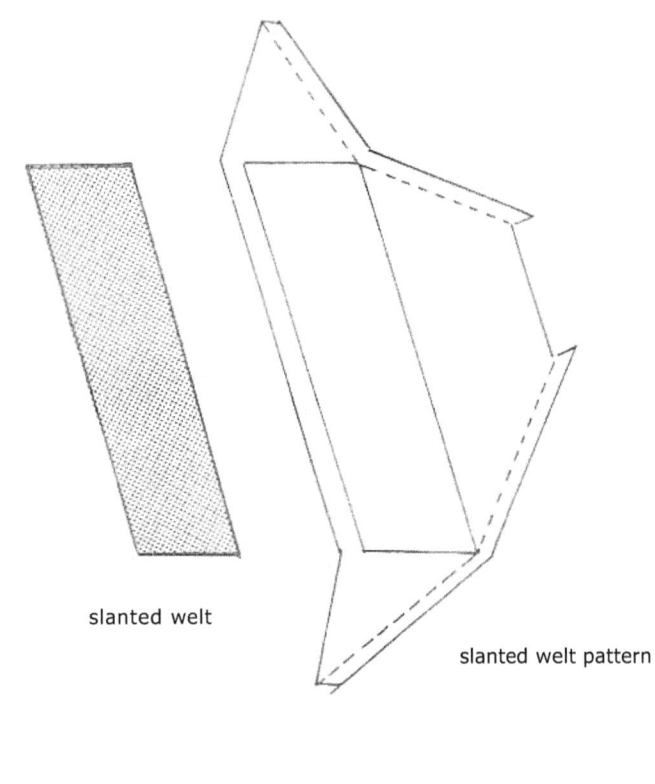
slanted welt

slanted welt pattern

Fig 164

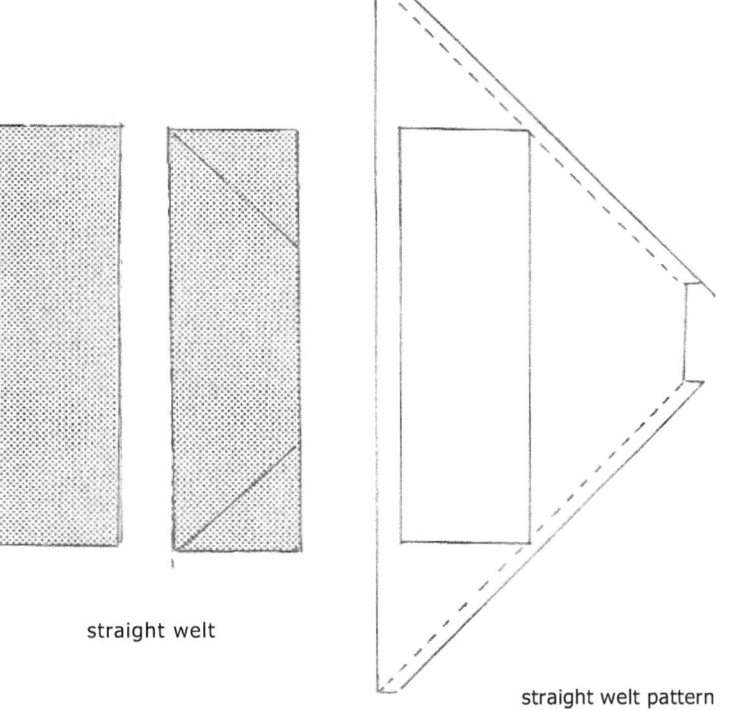
straight welt

straight welt pattern

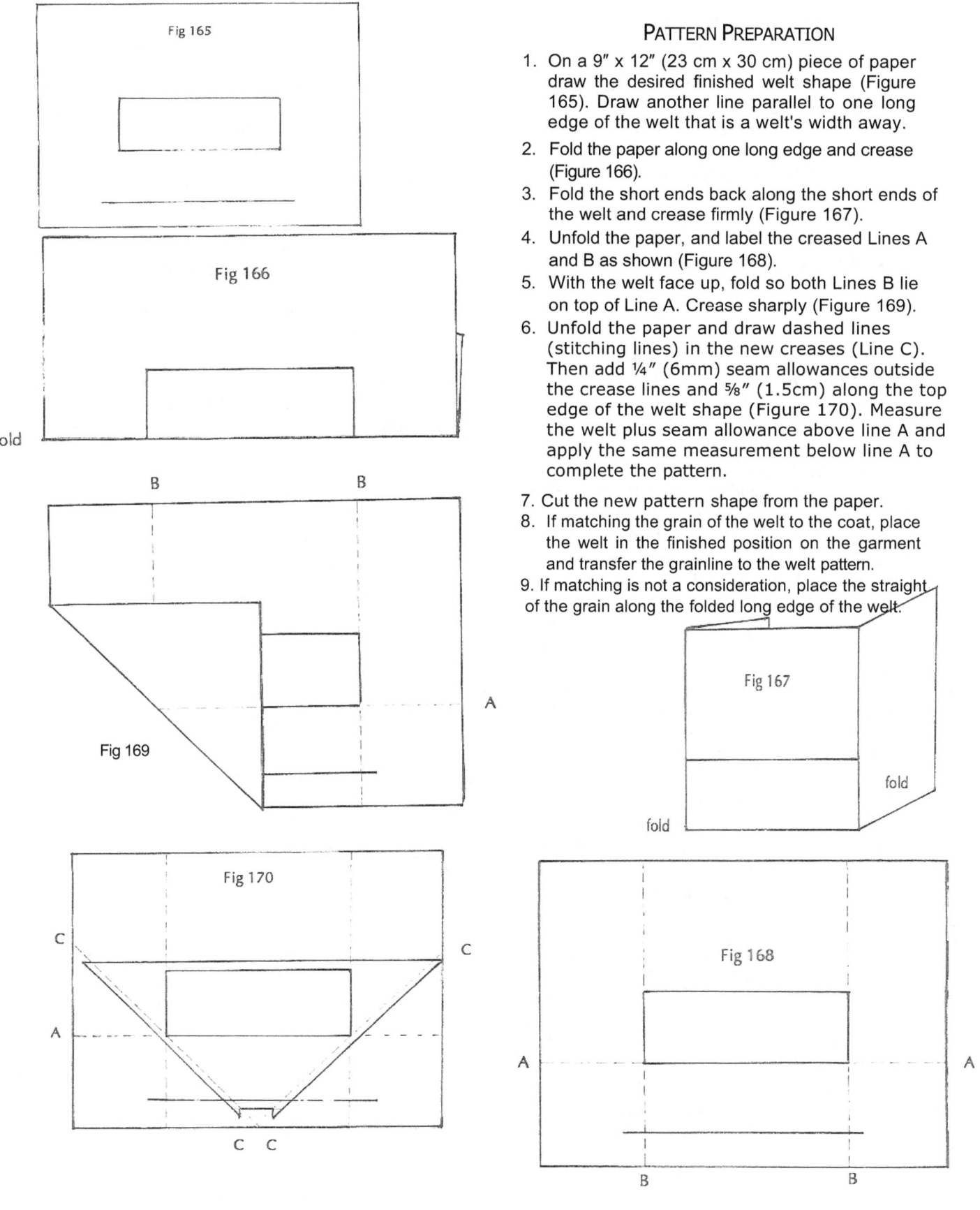

Pattern Preparation

1. On a 9" x 12" (23 cm x 30 cm) piece of paper draw the desired finished welt shape (Figure 165). Draw another line parallel to one long edge of the welt that is a welt's width away.
2. Fold the paper along one long edge and crease (Figure 166).
3. Fold the short ends back along the short ends of the welt and crease firmly (Figure 167).
4. Unfold the paper, and label the creased Lines A and B as shown (Figure 168).
5. With the welt face up, fold so both Lines B lie on top of Line A. Crease sharply (Figure 169).
6. Unfold the paper and draw dashed lines (stitching lines) in the new creases (Line C). Then add ¼" (6mm) seam allowances outside the crease lines and ⅝" (1.5cm) along the top edge of the welt shape (Figure 170). Measure the welt plus seam allowance above line A and apply the same measurement below line A to complete the pattern.
7. Cut the new pattern shape from the paper.
8. If matching the grain of the welt to the coat, place the welt in the finished position on the garment and transfer the grainline to the welt pattern.
9. If matching is not a consideration, place the straight of the grain along the folded long edge of the welt.

CUTTING

For each pocket, cut the following:

Welt: Use the new welt pattern piece to cut a welt from the fashion fabric. Also cut a welt from fusible or woven interfacing *in the exact size and shape of the finished welt.*

Pocket Bags: Cut two pocket bags from lining or pocketing fabric:, making one of them ⅝" smaller than the other along the straight edge.

Note: Lining fabric does not make satisfactory pocket bags in a heavy overcoat because of the differences in weight and hand between the two fabrics.

CONSTRUCTION

1. Apply interfacing to the wrong side of the welt.
2. With right sides together, stitch the mitered corners at each end of the welt, using ¼"-wide (6 mm) seam allowances. Press the seams open and turn the welt right side out.
3. To reinforce the pocket, cut a strip of fusible interfacing 2" wide and 1" longer than the pocket opening. Center over the pocket location marks on the wrong side of the coat and fuse in place.
4. Place the welt in position on the garment and mark the stitching lines and the end of the welt as shown, spacing the two long stitching lines parallel to each other and ⅝" (1.5 cm) apart (Figure 171).
5. Place the welt on the right side of the garment with the raw edges of the welt along the marked line closer to the side seam. Carefully lift the facing side of the welt out of the way and stitch only the face of the welt to the garment along the lower marked line (Figure 172).
6. Tuck the straight edge of the larger of the two pocket bags under the raw edges of the welt against the stitching. Fold the welt back onto the pocket bag and mark the short edges of the welt onto the bag (Figure 173).
7. Return the welt to its original position and stitch the bag to the garment, starting and ending one stitch inside the marks made in step 6. Be sure to backstitch carefully at each end (Figure 174). Cut the pocket opening between the two rows of stitching, slashing at an angle into the corners.
8. Press open the welt seam allowance, clip into the fold of the welt on each end from the raw edge to the stitching then push the welt seam allowance to the inside of the welt (Figure 175).
9. Baste the seam allowance on the facing side of the welt to the just-pressed seam allowance (Figure 176).
10. Place the smaller pocket bag face down on the welt with the straight raw edge even with the raw edges of the welt and garment seam allowance. Stitch through all layers—pocket bag, welt, and garment seam allowance—backstitch at the beginning and end of the seam at each end of the welt (Figure 177).
11. Pull the pocket bags through the pocket opening to the wrong side of the garment and stitch the outer edges of the pocket bags together. The small triangles at the welt ends should lie under the welt and point toward each other (Figure 178). (This differs from traditional methods where the triangle lies inside and you stitch over it to secure the end.)
12. If desired, topstitch or edgestitch the upper edge of the welt.
13. Attach the ends of the welt to the garment by edgestitching or by slipstitching by hand (Figure 178).

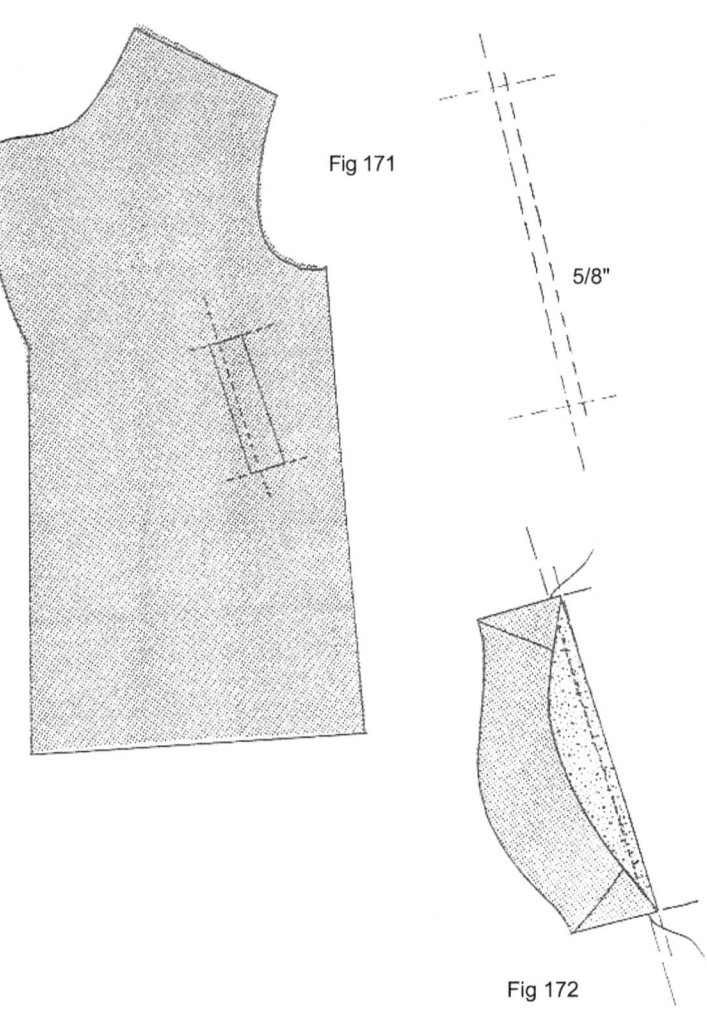

Fig 171

Fig 172

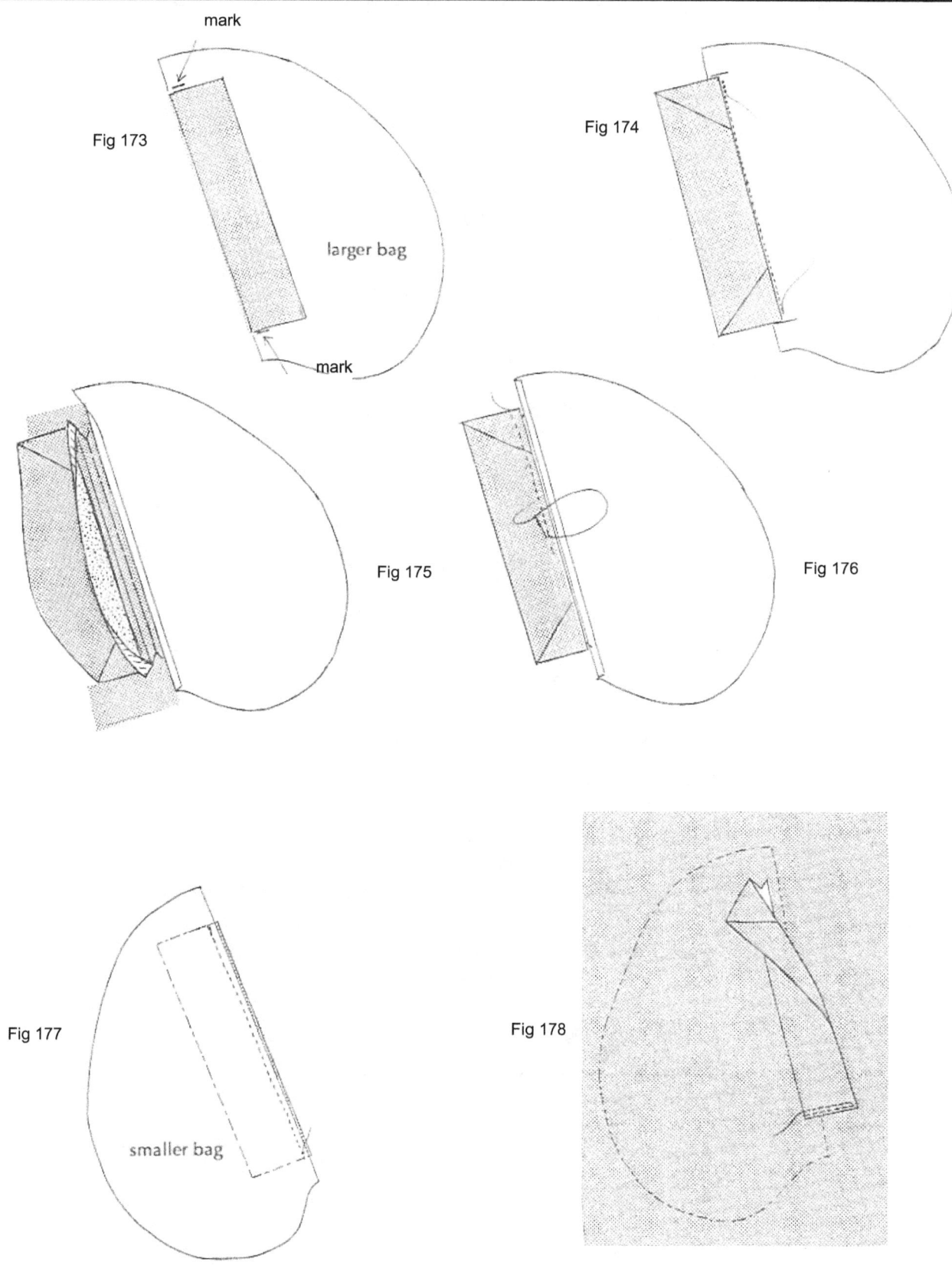

SOURCES

Things have changed a lot since this book was first published in 1994. Most suppliers now have a presence on the internet and search engines can help you home in on what you are looking for.

For items imported from Japan:

Professional Sewing Supplies
https://www.profsewingsupplies.com

BIBLIOGRAPHY

Bane, Allyne. *Tailoring.* McGraw-Hill. New York, NY, 1974.

—*Basic Tailoring.* Time/Life Books. New York, NY, 1973.

Hostek, Stanley. *Hand Stitches.* Seattle, WA, 1975.

Hostek, Stanley. *Men's Custom Tailored Coats.* Seattle, WA, 1972.

Lansing, Linda Thiel and Ledbetter, N. Marie. *Tailoring: Traditional and Contemporary Techniques.* Reston Publishing Company. Reston, VI, 1981.

—*Reader's Digest Complete Guide to Sewing.* The Reader's Digest Association, Inc., Pleasantville, NY, 1976.

—*Tailoring; Singer Sewing Library.* Cy DeCosse, Inc. Minnetonka, MN, 1988.

Three Pocket Patterns to copy and cutout

Slanted Welt Coat Pocket
Straight Welt Coat Pocket
Inside Coat Pocket

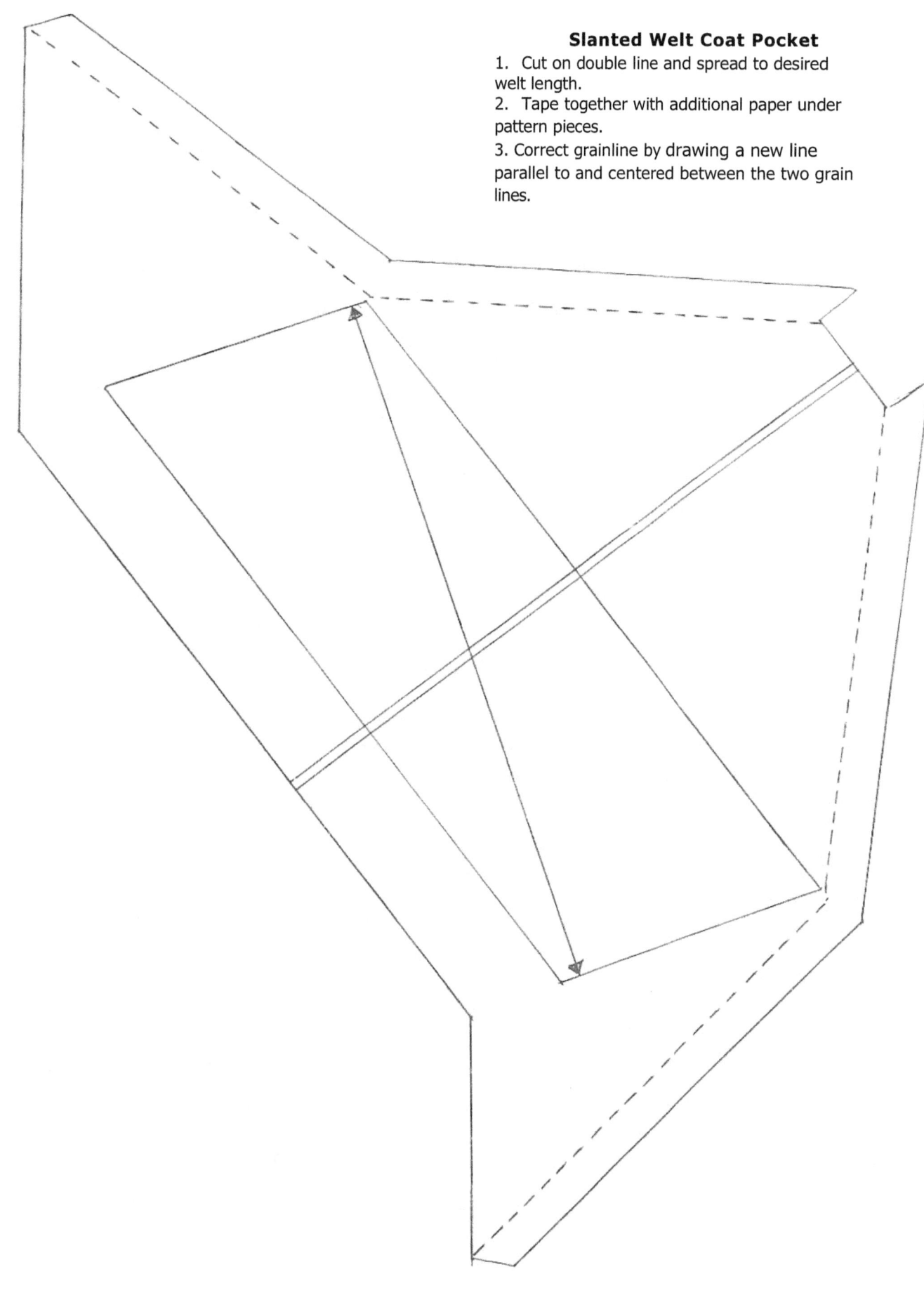

Slanted Welt Coat Pocket
1. Cut on double line and spread to desired welt length.
2. Tape together with additional paper under pattern pieces.
3. Correct grainline by drawing a new line parallel to and centered between the two grain lines.

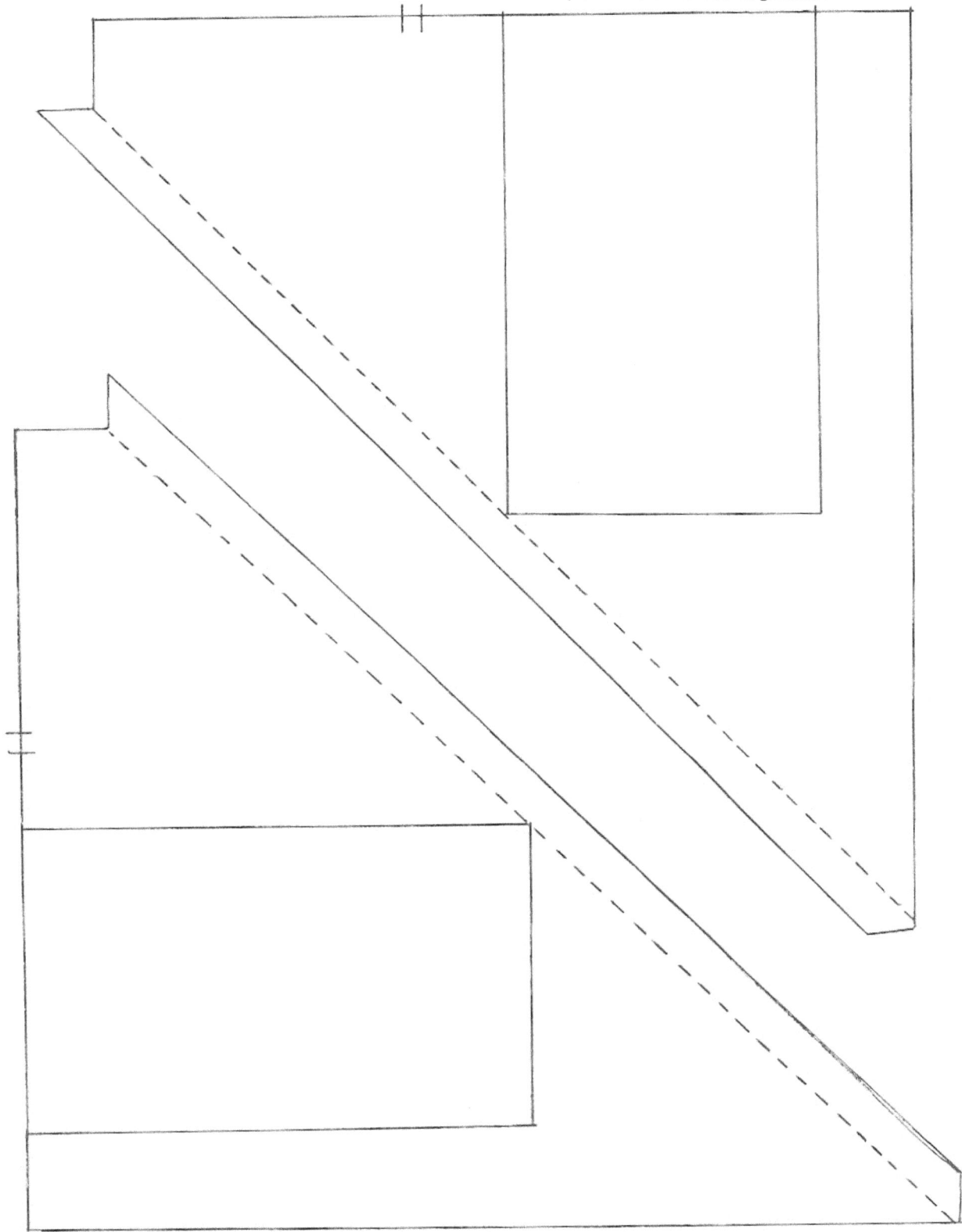

Straight Welt Coat Pocket
1. Cut out the 2 welt halves and butt together, matching notches.
2. Tape to hold halves together.

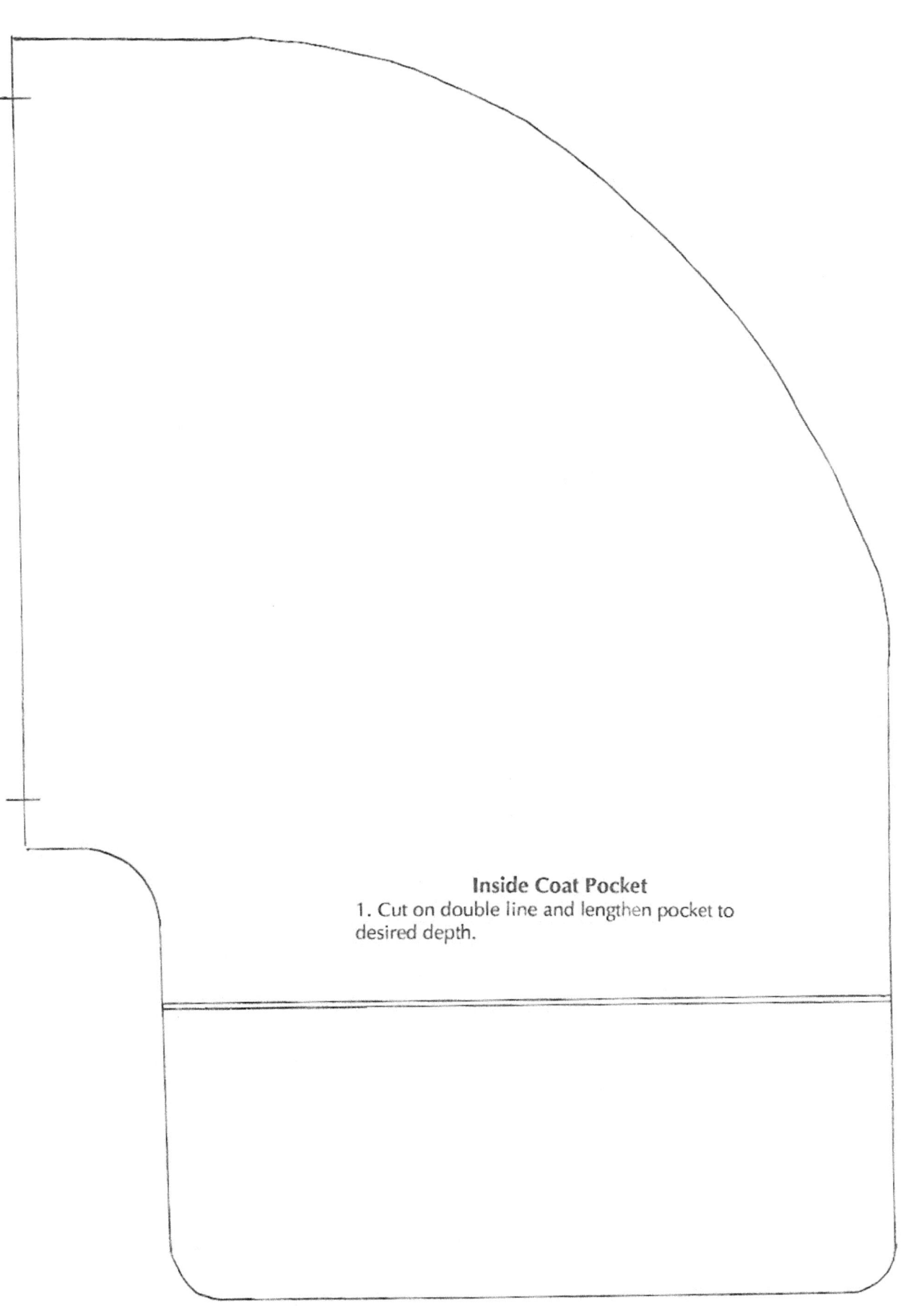

Inside Coat Pocket
1. Cut on double line and lengthen pocket to desired depth.

About the Author

Starr Miyeko Hashiguchi was born in 1929 in Auburn, Washington to Yoshio and Masaye Kakutani Urakawa, the oldest of four girls. During World War Two the family was imprisoned at the Minidoka War Relocation Center near Hunt, Idaho. Starr married Hachiro Hashiguchi in 1950. They had three children.

Her lifelong interest in the arts expressed itself professionally as well as in her hobbies: she taught sewing and tailoring at both Renton Vocational-Technical Institute, and Seattle Central Community College. She was also a seamstress with an extensive private clientele. She first self-published *Timeless Tailoring* in 1994 as a textbook. Later her talents extended to dollmaking, where her Japanese-styled sewn dolls were eagerly purchased at bazaars. She also was a gifted Hardanger embroider and taught classes in the art. Starr's own clothing, whether sewed, embroidered, knit, or crocheted, were works of art; and showed inspiration from both the traditional Japanese and the French designer Chanel.

Starr served as a Brownie and Girl Scout leader in the 1950s and 1960s inspiring many girls and young women.

An avid bowler in her youth, Starr was a devoted fan of all the Seattle professional sports teams: the Seahawks, the Mariners, and the SuperSonics, prior to their departure from Seattle.

Starr was quietly but cheerfully devout, first as a member of Japanese Congregational Church, and later serving for many years on boards and committees for Plymouth Congregational Church in Seattle.

In the latter part of her life, Starr traveled extensively and volunteered her time at the Keiro Rehabilitation and Care Center in Seattle.

Starr passed away in 2019. This second edition of her book was published in her memory.

www.ingramcontent.com/pod-product-compliance
Lightning Source LLC
Chambersburg PA
CBHW080739230426
43665CB00020B/2799